To Nicki, Juliana, and Greg

Acknowledgments

I'd like to thank the many people who helped me make this a better book. I first thank my wife, Nicki, who once again provided immense support throughout the entire project and proofread every page. She knows a lot about the subject and has been an invaluable assistant in helping the students in my GPS courses understand the concepts of outdoor navigation. I would also like to thank Lincoln Turner and Joe Mehaffey, two people who provided valuable information for earlier editions that continues to be important here. Lincoln's insight into traditional map-and-compass navigation has been especially valuable. Joe's wide knowledge of GPS, gained as co-owner of the website www.gpsinformation.net, also has been of immense help.

GPS technology continues to improve at a rapid rate, and I am indebted to several industry experts for keeping me up-to-date. Dr. Frank van Diggelen of Broadcom, author of a definitive book on such arcane subjects as Assisted GPS and Long Term Orbits, was immensely helpful in my quest to understand those topics. Charlie Conley and his technical experts at DeLorme gave me invaluable insight into the workings of the latest multichannel receivers.

On the production side, Roslyn Bullas, associate publisher at Wilderness Press, and Laura Shauger, my editor, have been a pleasure to work with. Their suggestions and support have done a lot to improve the final book. Finally, I would like to recognize those people within the industry whose help over the years has been invaluable: Jake Jacobson and Jessica Myers of Garmin, Steve Wegrzyn and Luke Morris of Lowrance, Michelle Wilkinson of National Geographic, Debby Chen of Magellan/ Fleishman-Hillard, Bryan Roth of Groundspeak, Inc., and Adriana De Paola of Revue Thommen AG.

Outdoor Navigation with GPS

Stephen W. Hinch

 **WILDERNESS PRESS** . . . *on the trail since 1967*

Outdoor Navigation with GPS

1st EDITION May 2004
2nd EDITION October 2007
3rd EDITION 2011

Copyright © 2004, 2007, and 2011 by Stephen W. Hinch

Front and back cover photos copyright © 2010 by Stephen W. Hinch
Interior photos, except where noted, by Stephen W. Hinch
Maps & illustrations: Stephen W. Hinch
Cover & interior design: Lisa Pletka
Layout: Larry B. Van Dyke
Editors: Roslyn Bullas and Laura Shauger

ISBN 978-0-89997-650-1

Manufactured in the United States of America

Published by: **Wilderness Press**
               Keen Communications
               2204 First Avenue South, Suite 102
               Birmingham, AL 35233
               (800) 443-7227
               info@wildernesspress.com
               www.wildernesspress.com

Visit our website for a complete listing of books and for ordering information.

Distributed by Publishers Group West

Cover photos: (top) Delicate Arch, Arches National Park: N38° 44.617´
               W109° 29.967´; *(bottom)* GPS receivers: Garmin GPSMAP 60CSx,
               DeLorme PN-40, Garmin Oregon 400t

SAFETY NOTICE: Although Wilderness Press and the author have made every attempt to ensure that the information in this book is accurate at press time, they are not responsible for any loss, damage, injury, or inconvenience that may occur to anyone while using this book or the products mentioned in this book. You are responsible for your own safety and health while in the wilderness. Be aware that the products covered here may have been updated or changed since this book was printed.

Contents

Preface

Not long ago, newspapers ran front-page articles about a hunter who had been lost for three days in snowy mountains during the middle of winter, supposedly because his GPS receiver had given him wrong directions. The only reason he survived was that he was accidentally discovered by a passing snowmobiler. Rangers who later tested his receiver found it was working fine; a more likely explanation was that he hadn't understood how to use it. But the story got wide publicity and did little to increase the public's confidence in GPS. Similar stories regularly make headlines. A driver in New York narrowly escaped death when he turned onto a railroad track in front of an oncoming train because his GPS receiver told him to turn. A family in Oregon was trapped overnight in snow because they followed the advice of their brand-new GPS receiver and took a "shortcut" over a remote Forest Service trail. In each case, the hapless travelers blamed their predicaments on GPS, not on themselves.

GPS manufacturers haven't exactly helped the situation. Their user manuals tend to be simple pamphlets that don't even explain all of the receiver's functions, let alone show you how to do anything useful like navigate to a destination and return safely. One of the most frequent laments in online reviews of GPS receivers is the lack of quality information in their user manuals.

You'd think that would worry GPS manufacturers. After all, newspaper headlines blaring, "Lost Hiker Found Dead Clutching GPS," don't do the industry any good. But you can't really blame the manufacturers. GPS is used in so many different ways, from hiking in the woods to navigating aircraft to coordinating artillery strikes, that it's not practical for a single instruction manual to cover all these uses and more.

To fill the gap, a thriving cottage industry of aftermarket books, videos, and hands-on instructional classes has emerged. But even here, you are likely to walk away confused. Many books treat GPS as an end in itself rather than as simply one tool to help you navigate. If your goal is to learn how to use GPS to find your way in the outdoors, you don't need to confuse things by learning how to do such things as survey an archaeological dig or dock a supertanker.

That's where this book comes in. It is written expressly for the outdoor navigator. You'll learn how to do the important things in a simple, easily understandable way. You'll learn how to keep from getting lost, how to navigate both simple and complex routes, and how to use your GPS receiver in conjunction with those two other venerable tools of wilderness navigation, the map and compass. You won't be overwhelmed trying to understand the countless other GPS features you're unlikely to ever need.

Fortunately, when it comes to outdoor navigation, using a GPS receiver is not all that complicated. That's true whether you're a hunter returning to your pickup after a day in the woods, a backpacker on a multiday trek, or a geocacher searching for hidden treasures in a local park. Don't worry if the instruction manual that came with your receiver doesn't show you how to navigate. You'll learn that here.

Which brings me to the next important topic: As I've said, GPS is used in many different ways. The subject of this book is recreational outdoor navigation. You'll see how to find your way in the backcountry, but not how to navigate ships or aircraft. If you really want to use GPS to do something dangerous like land an aircraft in a hailstorm or row solo across the Atlantic, you'll need expert instruction covering your specific needs.

TERMINOLOGY CLARIFICATION

Technically speaking, the term "GPS" describes the entire Global Positioning System. What you hold in your hand is a "GPS receiver." Lots of people just call it a "GPS," but I'll try to avoid that here. A slang term to describe a GPS receiver that's gained popularity in the geocaching community is "GPSr." It remains to be seen how widely it will be adopted, so I won't use it. If you want to understand the many other GPS-related terms, read the glossary at the back of the book.

There are dozens of GPS receivers on the market today, and this book can't cover everything about all of them. Instead, this book introduces the concepts of GPS navigation and illustrates them with the kinds of receivers used in the outdoors. That way, you can use what you learn regardless of which receiver you own today or which one you might buy next year.

Throughout this book are screen shots from numerous receivers from several manufacturers. Some are taken from receivers I own. Others come from ones manufacturers loaned to me expressly for this book. These screen shots can only serve as examples. It's not practical to explain the exact button sequences for every receiver out there. So don't throw away that instruction manual—you'll still need it. But the examples here should help you make more sense out of your own GPS unit.

No book can ever be a substitute for experience. Before you go charging off on that once-in-a-lifetime solo hike to the South Pole, get plenty of practice on lesser challenges. Spend some time using your receiver in the yard, around the neighborhood, in nearby parks—places where if you make a mistake, you won't need a search-and-rescue team to retrieve you. My strong words of advice are that until you are completely comfortable with GPS and can routinely navigate without making mistakes, don't use it to go anywhere you can't find your way back from without it.

Remember, a GPS receiver is a complex electronic instrument. While it's fairly rugged, it's not indestructible. Batteries can run down, it can get damaged from rough handling, or you can lose it off a 100-foot cliff. Before you start out on any serious wilderness exploration, make sure you carry a map and compass and know how to use them. Although this book doesn't cover everything you want to know about map-and-compass navigation, it gives you enough information to get by in a pinch.

If you want to know how to use GPS for recreational adventures such as hiking, backpacking, hunting, fishing, river rafting, kayaking, mountain biking, snowshoeing, outdoor photography, or the fast-growing sport of geocaching, this book is for you. The focus is on practical applications, not technical theory. You'll learn how to be successful and safe, and how to get the most enjoyment out of your investment. The theory covered in these pages is limited to what you need to know to achieve success. If you really want to delve into the gory technical details of such things as satellite PRN sequences or dilution-of-precision errors, there are plenty of advanced textbooks and websites to keep you occupied for months.

You don't even need to own a GPS receiver to get something out of this book. In fact, if you're thinking of making the investment but haven't yet done so, this book can help you make the best choice. Even if your partner is more interested in GPS than you are, you might want to pick up a copy. My wife never showed much interest in GPS until one day when she discovered the sport of geocaching. Now she's as likely to pull me along on an outdoor treasure hunt as I am to lead her into the backcountry. Geocaching is a great sport for the whole family, combining elements of a treasure hunt, outdoor exercise, and navigation skills in a form that helps you quickly gain GPS experience.

This book is organized into four parts, starting with the basics and building from there. Part I gives you the background behind what GPS is and how it is used. You'll learn what to look for in a GPS receiver and how to do basic things like marking and going to waypoints and following compass bearings.

Part II introduces the concepts of latitude and longitude, and how to use them to find a place you've never been to before. You'll learn the UTM system, an alternative to latitude and longitude developed by the military that has advantages for hikers and backpackers. This is also where you will learn about topographic maps and how to read waypoint coordinates from both paper and software maps.

Part III describes the critical wilderness navigation skills you should know if your GPS receiver fails in the backcountry. You will not only learn basic map-and-compass navigation but also more primitive techniques and methods for avoiding disaster in the first place.

Part IV, which covers such topics as geocaching, geotagging, GPS games, trail mapping, and highway navigation, shows you how to get the most out of your GPS receiver. You'll also discover the latest in equipment offerings from major manufacturers. Finally, two appendices and a glossary provide answers to frequently asked questions.

GPS has rightfully been called the greatest advance in navigation since the invention of the compass. Even if you never expect to use it for anything more complicated than getting back to your car in a crowded parking lot, you'll find it helpful. And once you know how to do that, it won't be long before you'll want to do more. Whatever your intended use, this book will help you get the most from your GPS receiver.

Stephen W. Hinch
Santa Rosa, California

Part I
Basic Navigation

Key Concepts

▶ History of GPS

▶ How it works

▶ The four essential GPS skills

▶ Features of GPS receivers

▶ GPS limitations

▶ Waypoint basics

▶ Bearings: What they are and how to follow them

▶ MARK and GOTO: The two most Important GPS functions

▶ All about compasses

▶ The difference between true and magnetic north

Basics of GPS

The Global Positioning System has revolutionized the art of finding your way in the outdoors. Whether you are a backpacker on a multiday trek or a mountain biker out for an afternoon ride, GPS can help you reach your destination and return safely anywhere on earth, thanks to a system of two dozen satellites funded and maintained by the U.S. government that orbit silently overhead.

The idea of using satellites for navigation has been around since at least the late 1950s, when those few satellites in orbit were still the size of basketballs and neither the U.S. nor the USSR had yet launched a man into space. Throughout the 1960s, the U.S. Army, Navy, and Air Force all worked on various competing and incompatible systems. Government bureaucracy being what it is, the Department of Defense didn't decide until 1973 to combine all these efforts into a single program. Much to the

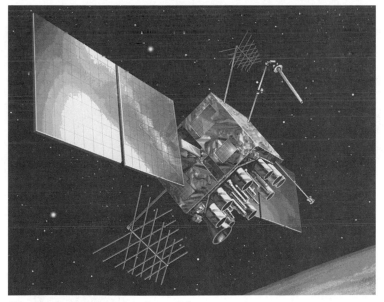

GPS satellite (Lockheed Martin Space Systems Co.)

Navy's chagrin, the Air Force got the nod to lead the development and operation of the new system, dubbed the Navstar Global Positioning System. Nowadays we call it GPS.

Work progressed rapidly once the efforts were unified. The first prototype satellite was launched in 1978 and second-generation production versions were launched starting in 1989. The system was declared fully operational in 1995, after the last of the 24 second-generation satellites was deployed. The satellites have operational lives of between 3 and 10 years, so new ones are launched regularly to replace older ones before they go out of service.

GPS first gained worldwide fame in 1991 during Operation Desert Storm, the conflict that also brought us night-vision goggles and the Hummer. The viewing public was quickly captured by television images of armored units being guided with pinpoint accuracy across a featureless Iraqi desert. GPS was so useful in Desert Storm that the military soon ran out of receivers for the troops and had to buy more than 10,000 consumer GPS units to make up the difference.

The fact that there were even consumer GPS receivers for the military to buy was not always a given. The military had imagined all sorts of ways GPS could be used against us by our enemies, and they were dubious about letting the technology loose on the public. But the 1983 downing of Korean Air Flight 007 by the Soviet Union removed any doubt. This tragedy arose in part because the 747's flight crew made a navigation error, and the xenophobic Russians shot them down. GPS, if it had been available, could have prevented that fatal mistake. As a result, President Ronald Reagan issued a directive that GPS signals be free and available to the entire world, and the commercial market has flourished ever since.

But the military was still wary. From the outset, they planned for two versions of the system: a high-accuracy version available only to the military and a separate civilian version whose accuracy could be degraded without affecting military operations. In the early years, they degraded the accuracy of the civilian system through a process known as Selective Availability, or SA. This artificial degradation reduced the accuracy from an inherent 50-foot capability to something around 300 feet—the length of a football field.

For wilderness navigation, a 300-foot error isn't catastrophic. If you can get within a few hundred feet of your destination, you ought to be able to figure out the rest of the way on your own. But for aircraft and ships, it could mean disaster. Predictably, SA caused considerable public outcry, particularly from commercial users. The U.S. Coast Guard and others even deployed their own enhancement to the system, called

Differential GPS, which could eliminate the effects of SA to help ships safely navigate through harbors.

Finally, after numerous studies and substantial lobbying, President Bill Clinton ordered that SA be permanently turned off beginning May 2, 2000. The improvement since that time has been remarkable. While the stated accuracy of civilian GPS is about 50 feet, most of the time you can find your position to within 20 feet or less. In the meantime, the military figured out how to locally degrade the accuracy of civilian GPS wherever in the world they're currently doing battle, without affecting it for the rest of us.

How GPS Works

GPS works by the process of triangulation. (Technically, it is called trilateration because it calculates your position using distances rather than angles, but the concept is similar, and the terms are often used interchangeably.) It's the same theme you've seen in countless World War II movies. The heroic French resistance fighter hides in a farmhouse, using his clandestine radio transmitter to send vital military secrets to the Allies. All the while, the Nazis are driving around in a big truck, listening in and trying to pinpoint his position. They invariably find him, but not until after he has broadcast the critical information.

In this scenario, the Nazis are using a technique called radio direction finding. With a radio receiver and an antenna that's very sensitive to the direction it's pointed, you can determine the direction a radio transmission is coming from. If you take readings from several different locations and plot them on a map, you'll find the transmitter at the location where all the lines intersect.

GPS is similar, with one significant difference. Instead of measuring the direction to each GPS satellite, your receiver determines its distance from each of them. It does this by measuring the time it takes to receive each of their signals. Knowing the travel time of the signals and the speed of light, it can determine the distance to each satellite. It then has to figure out the precise location of each satellite in the sky. For this, it uses accurate information about satellite orbits stored in its internal memory. Once it knows the locations and distances of at least three satellites, your receiver has everything it needs to calculate your position. The math is a little complicated, but that's something for your GPS receiver to worry about.

This process only works if your receiver knows exactly when each satellite sent its signal and exactly when it was received, so accurate time is an essential part of the system. All GPS satellites carry atomic clocks synchronized to three billionths of a second. Your handheld

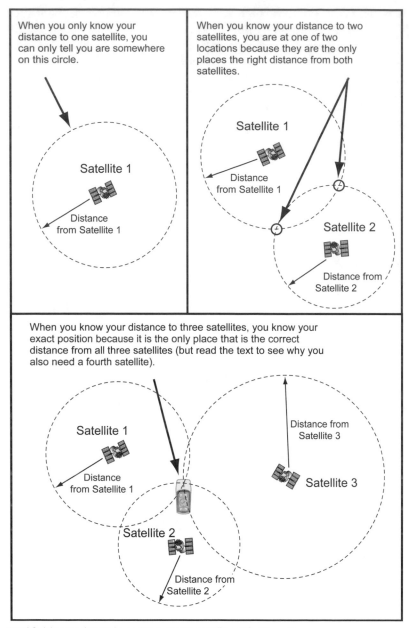

When you only know your distance to one satellite, you can only tell you are somewhere on this circle.

Satellite 1

Distance from Satellite 1

When you know your distance to two satellites, you are at one of two locations because they are the only places the right distance from both satellites.

Satellite 1

Distance from Satellite 1

Satellite 2

Distance from Satellite 2

When you know your distance to three satellites, you know your exact position because it is the only place that is the correct distance from all three satellites (but read the text to see why you also need a fourth satellite).

Satellite 1

Distance from Satellite 1

Satellite 2

Distance from Satellite 2

Distance from Satellite 3

Satellite 3

Simplified diagram showing how a GPS receiver uses satellites to find its position receiver, of course, doesn't include such a clock, but it doesn't need to. By tracking a fourth satellite, it can calculate its position multiple ways using all combinations of three satellites. This "redundancy" gives it enough information to eliminate the error in its internal clock. Without that extra satellite, your receiver won't be nearly as accurate; in some cases it could be in error by more than a mile. By the way, this ability to lock onto atomic clocks makes your GPS receiver the most accurate timepiece you can readily buy.

Parts of the System

There are three parts to the GPS system: the satellite segment, the user segment, and the control segment.

Satellite segment. Satellites are the heart of the Global Positioning System. They broadcast the signals your receiver uses to determine your position. (Chapter 2 looks at the different types of signals in more detail.) At least 24 satellites are in operation at all times, each orbiting the earth every 12 hours (or 11 hours and 58 minutes, if you want to be precise). Their orbits are designed so that, theoretically, at least 6 and as many as 12 satellites are above the horizon virtually all the time, regardless of where you are. "Theoretically" is the key word here—the satellite signals don't travel through mountains, buildings, people, or heavy tree cover, so unless you're on a flat plain or body of water, some signals probably will be blocked. Since your receiver must lock onto at least four satellites to accurately determine its position, you may have to move around to get better reception. (By the way, it's a little-known fact that all GPS satellites perform a second duty: Each includes an X-ray detector that lets the U.S. government monitor nuclear explosions anywhere in the world.)

User segment. Your handheld receiver makes up the user segment. There's a lot of power inside that little package. Not only does it contain a sensitive receiver capable of detecting signals less than a quadrillionth the power of a light bulb, it also includes a powerful computer that converts the raw data into such useful information as your position and speed. A GPS receiver doesn't include any kind of transmitter, meaning it is a passive positioning system—you can determine your own position, but there's no way for anyone else to use it to track you.

Control segment. This part keeps the whole system running smoothly. Satellites need to be kept in their proper orbits and their signal transmissions kept up-to-date. The Air Force operates a series of five ground stations around the globe, typically at exotic tropical locations: Hawaii,

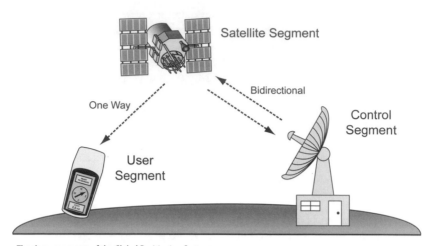

The three segments of the Global Positioning System

Ascension Island, Diego Garcia, Kwajalein, and the decidedly nontropical master station in Colorado Springs. You'll probably never think about the control segment, but without it, the entire system would quickly fall into disrepair.

GPS Accuracy

How accurate is the GPS system? It's surprisingly difficult to get a good answer to that question. Some sources say a consumer GPS receiver is accurate to within 100 feet. Others report it as 50 feet. Manufacturers often give even better numbers, in the vicinity of 20 feet or less. What's the true story?

First, don't depend on your receiver to tell you. Although many receivers report something called "Estimated Position Error" or EPE, it is not very accurate. This estimate is based only on satellite geometry and doesn't consider the various other sources of error. Second, remember that until May 2, 2000, Selective Availability was the most significant source of error. Anything you read that was published before then is probably out-of-date.

The next thing to do is see what the Department of Defense says. After all, they operate the system, so they ought to know its performance, right? But they aren't as much help as you'd wish. In a typically conservative fashion, they don't specify total system accuracy, only the part within their direct control, which they call the Signal-in-Space, or SIS. It defines the accuracy of the signals as they radiate from the satellites but leaves out errors introduced as the signals propagate through the atmosphere.

Unfortunately, ever since the demise of Selective Availability, the atmosphere—especially the ionosphere—is the most significant source of GPS error. Just as the moon and sun look distorted as they drop low in the sky, signals from GPS satellites are bent as they travel through the atmosphere. They also experience delays that vary depending on the time of day, current solar activity, and moisture level in the air. Manufacturers of GPS receivers use mathematical models to predict and compensate for these errors, but atmospheric conditions are never constant.

The Defense Department estimates the accuracy of civilian GPS units to be better than 50 feet at least 95 percent of the time, anywhere in the world. This is what's called the 2drms (twice the distance root-mean-square) accuracy. It is based on statistics. Don't worry about the math. Just remember that the 2drms number means that over an entire day, a receiver's accuracy should be better than 50 feet at least 95 percent of the time.

Not all manufacturers specify their receivers this way. Some specify a simple rms value, which is half the 2drms number. Although the number looks smaller, you will only see this accuracy two-thirds of the time. Still others report a Circular Error Probable, or CEP. This is an even smaller number, but you will only be that close to your destination half the time. By specifying simple rms or CEP, manufacturers can make the numbers look better, but the receiver may not be any more accurate. The 2drms accuracy is a conservative number. It's twice as large as simple rms and 2.4 times larger than CEP accuracy for the same receiver.

Another unpredictable effect is called multipath error. Satellite signals are reflected by such obstacles as tall buildings or canyon walls, which can confuse your receiver as it determines its distance from a satellite. Unfortunately, there's not much a receiver manufacturer can do to eliminate this error. You have to move your receiver away from the offending object.

If the government claims only 50-foot 2drms accuracy, you might wonder how manufacturers can claim better performance. Two factors come into play. First, the 50-foot number is a very conservative estimate that applies anywhere in the world. You would probably see such performance only on rare occasions. Second, manufacturers continue to improve their software models of the ionospheric effect, so today's receivers are slightly more accurate than those produced a few years ago.

In reality, consumer receivers will get you to within about 25 feet of your intended destination most of the time. While manufacturers will undoubtedly continue to improve their software, you won't see much more improvement without the help of DGPS or WAAS, two enhancements described in the next section.

Civilian receivers operate on a single frequency, called L1, at 1575.42 megahertz. Single-frequency receivers are susceptible to the effects of the ionosphere as explained above. Military receivers use both L1 and a second frequency called L2, at 1227.6 megahertz. This second frequency contains an encrypted code available only to the military that allows the receiver to eliminate ionospheric error. In 2005, the Defense Department began launching a new series of satellites that will give civilians access to a second signal called L2C. When fully deployed in 2012, it will allow consumer receivers to also eliminate ionospheric error, but you'll need a new GPS receiver to take advantage of this improvement. A third civilian signal called L5, at 1176.45 megahertz, will provide even higher accuracy for safety-of-life applications such as aircraft navigation.

There are a few things you can do to improve the accuracy of your measurements. First, try to make sure your receiver has a clear view of the sky and is tracking at least four satellites. More than four is even better—your receiver uses the extra satellites to further refine the accuracy of its measurements. Second, if your receiver has an "averaging" function, use it. (Usually, you'll find it labeled something like AVG as a selection on the MARK page.) The averaging function allows your receiver to accumulate many measurements over time and average them. Since GPS errors tend to be random, the longer you average, the more accurate your position. To be useful, you need to average for at least several minutes, and you must stay in one position during that period. Finally, although you can't depend on the EPE readout on your receiver to be truly accurate, it is a good relative indicator. Smaller numbers are better than larger numbers.

Finally, there is a difference between how accurately a receiver can determine its position and how accurately it will take you back to that position later. To understand why, refer to the diagram here. Suppose you want to record the coordinates of Position A, where you have just placed a hidden geocache. Because your receiver can only determine your position to within about 25 feet,

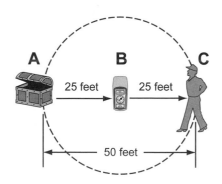

The error in returning to a previously marked waypoint is worse than the error in finding your absolute position.

the coordinates it gives you might be those of Position B, 25 feet away from the true location. When you mark the position as Waypoint A, you are actually storing the coordinates of where your GPS receiver thinks it is—Position B—not where you actually are, Position A.

When you later want to find the geocache, you tell your receiver to go to Waypoint A. It will actually try to guide you to its stored location, Position B. But once again, because of system inaccuracies, you can only get to within perhaps 25 feet of that location. Depending on your luck, you could end up right on the treasure or as far away as Position C, which is 25 feet away from Position B and 50 feet away from your intended destination. You are unlikely to ever encounter this worst-case example. A more realistic estimate takes the receiver's specified accuracy and multiplies it by a factor of 1.4, which suggests you should routinely be able to return to within 35 feet of a previously stored location. But remember that once in awhile, your error will fall outside this estimate.

Improving GPS Accuracy: DGPS and WAAS

Today's basic 50-foot accuracy is sufficient for outdoor recreation, but it's still marginal for certain commercial uses, primarily involving air or sea navigation. Two enhancements have been made to improve system accuracy in certain situations. The first is the Coast Guard's Differential GPS, or DGPS. Although initially intended to guide ships on navigable waterways, it now extends to highway navigation. The Coast Guard operates more than 60 ground stations throughout the country, and the position of each has been accurately surveyed. Inside each station is a GPS receiver that compares the known location of the station with its position as measured by GPS. The difference is broadcast as a set of correction factors your receiver can use to improve its accuracy. DGPS allows you to reduce errors to just a few feet of uncertainty.

Unfortunately, to receive DGPS correction signals, you need a separate, specialized receiver connected to your main GPS receiver. The additional DGPS receiver, together with its antenna, is so large you need a backpack to carry it, making it impractical for wilderness navigators. You also need to be within range of a ground station, so the technique has limited geographical coverage.

Another enhancement that's getting a lot of publicity these days is the Wide Area Augmentation System, or WAAS. It consists of 38 ground stations throughout North America as well as several satellites in high-altitude geostationary orbits over the equator. Strictly speaking, WAAS refers to the system covering North America. The more general term is Satellite Based Augmentation System, or SBAS. Sometimes it's called

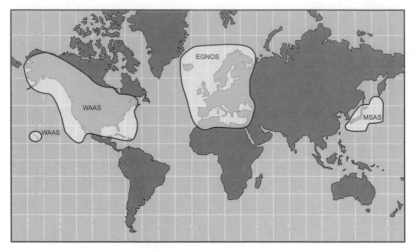

WAAS, EGNOS, and MSAS are all designed to improve the accuracy of civilian GPS.

Wide Area DGPS, or WADGPS. The equivalent system in Europe is called EGNOS, while in Japan it is called MSAS.

Similar to DGPS, the ground stations measure the performance of the GPS system and determine correction factors that eliminate errors arising from current atmospheric conditions and system timing variations. Unlike DGPS, which broadcasts the correction factors from ground stations, WAAS corrections are sent to the geostationary satellites, which then broadcast them to your receiver. Again, accuracies of a few feet are achievable. Many newer GPS units can receive WAAS corrections without any additional equipment, making it more attractive than DGPS.

WAAS was designed primarily for aircraft navigation, although a lot of the publicity makes it sound like a panacea for all ills. However, it's not all that useful for wilderness navigators. Only two satellites are visible from the U.S., and they're both low in the southern sky. Although this condition isn't a problem for aircraft, in many areas of the country, the satellites aren't reliably visible from the ground. Another variant, Local Area Augmentation System, or LAAS, is designed to guide aircraft on final approach and landing, and consequently operates only in the immediate vicinity of major airports.

Don't worry about using DGPS, WAAS, or LAAS in the outdoors. In fact, if you have a WAAS-enabled receiver, you may be better off disabling that feature and conserving battery power. I've never needed WAAS accuracy to find hidden geocaches, which is probably the most exacting recreational use of GPS you're likely to do.

OTHER GPS-LIKE SYSTEMS

The fact that GPS is operated by the U.S. Department of Defense causes concern in some countries. Several other GPS-like systems are currently being developed.

GLONASS is a Russian system that, like GPS, offers both civilian and military versions. When fully operational, GLONASS will consist of 24 satellites in three different orbital planes. As of 2009, about two-thirds of the satellites were operational, with full operation not scheduled until after 2010.

Another system, GALILEO, is being developed in Europe. It was originally intended as a fee-based service operated by private companies, but the developers soon realized this would be uncompetitive with the freely-available GPS system. GALILEO will now be a free service funded by the European Union. GALILEO is not expected to be fully operational until at least 2013. GPS, GLONASS, and GALILEO are all intended to be compatible; with the right receiver, you will be able to determine your position using any of the satellites visible from your current location.

A fourth system is being developed by the Chinese government. Their initial system, called BEIDOU-1, will use a small number of geostationary satellites to provide local coverage in China. The follow-on system, called BEIDOU-2 or COMPASS, will use medium-earth orbit satellites to provide worldwide coverage. The Chinese government has announced very little about these systems, and full deployment is probably many years away. Other specialized systems are in the early stages of development in India, France, and Japan.

GPS in the Wilderness: Essential Skills

In the simplest sense, a GPS receiver measures your exact position anywhere on earth, but navigation in the wilderness involves much more than knowing where you are. Now is a good time to introduce what I call the cardinal rule of GPS navigation: *It doesn't do you any good to know where you are if you don't know where you want to go.*

The real contribution of GPS isn't showing you where you are, but showing how to get where you want to go. The problem is complicated by the fact that GPS receivers report numerous other pieces of information besides your current position. How do you know what's important and what isn't?

First remember that all GPS receivers really only measure three things: your position, your speed, and the current time. (More expensive receivers sometimes include a true magnetic compass and barometric altimeter, but these are separate instruments that don't use GPS to make their measurements.) All the other features—things like distance, bearing, map location, and even such vital details as sunrise and sunset or the best fishing times—are calculations your receiver makes from those three measurements. That's why even the least expensive units work fine for outdoor navigators. They might not offer a lot of extras, but they all do the few things you really want.

So what are those few things? For outdoor navigation, there are only four things you should really know how to do with your GPS receiver. If you can do these, you can successfully navigate in the wilderness. They are:

▶ Know how to store your current location in GPS memory, a process referred to as marking a waypoint.

▶ Know how to get back to that stored location from wherever you might be. You'll do this by following a bearing.

▶ Know how to program into your GPS receiver the coordinates of locations you want to go to, a process referred to as entering a waypoint.

▶ Know how to navigate from one stored waypoint to the next in succession until you get to your final destination, a process referred to as following a route.

It's as simple as that. If you know how to do those four things, you'll be able to get where you want to go and return safely. Most of the rest of this book shows you how to do them. It also discusses what to do if your GPS receiver fails. And to keep all this knowledge from going to waste, it ends with some fun things to do with GPS.

THE FOUR ESSENTIAL GPS SKILLS

▶ Store your current location as a GPS waypoint.

▶ Return to a stored waypoint by following a bearing.

▶ Program waypoint latitudes and longitudes into your GPS receiver.

▶ Navigate from one waypoint to the next in succession until you reach your final destination.

GPS Receivers

You can buy a GPS receiver to fit almost any budget, from a basic, entry-level product for less than $100 to a deluxe model costing many hundreds of dollars. Not all of them are suitable for exploring the backcountry. In this chapter, you learn what you need to know about GPS receivers for the outdoors —what features are essential, which are merely nice, and what to avoid. First, though, you need to learn a bit more about how receivers work.

Satellite Signals

As you learned in Chapter 1, a GPS receiver works by measuring its distance from each of at least four satellites. Because it knows the exact location of each satellite, your receiver can calculate its position anywhere on earth, a process known as obtaining a position fix. But before it can do so, your receiver needs quite a bit of information from each satellite: its precise orbit, the time delay between when the satellite signal was sent and when it was received, and the exact GPS time. Each satellite broadcasts

Tools of the outdoor navigator: map, compass, and GPS receiver

several types of data. Once you see how this all works, you'll understand why your receiver sometimes gets a position fix right away and other times takes a lot longer.

Your receiver needs different types of data to calculate its position:

Almanac data. Although there are always at least 24 satellites in the sky, their orbits are such that not all are simultaneously visible from any one location on earth. As few as six and as many as 12 may be visible from your present location. It's hard enough for your receiver to detect signals that are actually there. To reduce the time wasted looking for satellites on the other side of the globe, your receiver stores a table of information about satellite orbits, called almanac data, which it uses to predict which satellites should be visible from your current position. It's not very precise information, but it's good enough to tell which satellites are above the horizon.

Your receiver gets its almanac data from the satellites themselves. Each satellite broadcasts the complete almanac for the entire array of 24 satellites, so you only need to connect to one satellite to collect that information. Once your receiver has loaded a current almanac, the information stays valid for about six months. It's a good thing, too, because if you let the almanac get out-of-date by not using your receiver for an extended period, it takes at least 12.5 minutes to download a new one. If you ever find yourself in this situation, turn your receiver on, set it in a place where it has a clear view of the sky, and go have dinner. When you return, it should be finished downloading the new almanac—a process known as initialization.

You may also have to initialize your receiver if you've moved more than a few hundred miles from your last position. If you're in San Francisco and the last time you used it was in London, your receiver will still look for satellites that are above the horizon in London. After unsuccessfully searching for a few minutes, it may ask you to input the state or country you're in, and perhaps what time it is, before it can find its position.

Ephemeris data. Almanac data is not accurate enough for your receiver to determine your exact distance from a satellite. For this, your receiver needs very accurate satellite orbital information. Each satellite broadcasts information about its own orbit, called ephemeris data, which takes about 30 seconds to download. Your receiver needs ephemeris data from at least four satellites before it can find its position, so it can take as long as two minutes to acquire the necessary information. Most receivers can speed the process by downloading from multiple satellites at once, reducing the total time to less than a minute. Ephemeris data

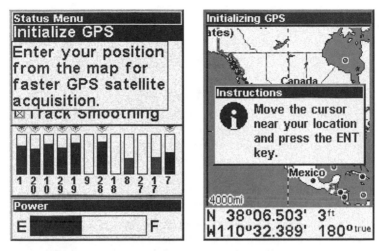

Mapping receivers like this Lowrance iFinder H2Oc make initialization easier by allowing you to move a pointer to your approximate position on the map screen.

stays valid for a few hours, so as long as you turn on your receiver occasionally during the day, you won't have to wait for this information to reload when you're ready to use it.

PRN code. This is the signal your receiver uses to measure the transmission time delay from each satellite. Civilian GPS units use a binary code that's 1023 bits long and takes 1 millisecond to transmit. (Military GPS uses a code that is six days long and much harder to jam.) PRN, which stands for "pseudo-random noise," is a noiselike signal that is relatively easy to detect and fairly difficult to jam.

Your receiver tracks these signals on up to 12 satellites simultaneously. But that's not all. The job is made even more difficult because all 24 satellites broadcast this information on exactly the same frequency. To understand the challenge this presents, think of it this way. Suppose you've settled down in front of your TV to watch a rerun of your favorite TV show, *Friends*. But your TV isn't quite working properly, so when you turn it on, not only do you see *Friends*, you also get a ghost image of *Gilligan's Island* from the adjacent channel. Your job is to follow what's going on with Rachel and Ross while ignoring what's going on between the Professor and Mary Ann.

Your GPS receiver has a similar task, but the analogy is that instead of ignoring *Gilligan's Island*, it is enjoying both shows simultaneously. In fact, it's not really happy unless it's watching at least four shows, and it can watch up to 12 shows at once without losing track of what any of the characters in any of the shows is doing. It's the goal every good couch potato strives for—watching a dozen shows at once without ever having to use the remote control to switch between them!

Acquisition Time

The length of time it takes your receiver to find its position depends on how long it's been since you last used it. Manufacturers often specify acquisition time using terms like "cold start," "warm start," and "hot start." Although all manufacturers don't always define them exactly the same way, the following are typical:

Cold start. Your receiver must perform a cold start when it has valid almanac data but no valid ephemeris data. In this case, it takes between 45 seconds and two minutes to find its position. Your receiver must perform a cold start if it hasn't been used in more than six hours but less than six months, when its almanac data expires.

Warm start. In this case, your receiver has valid almanac data, but the ephemeris data is valid only for three satellites. It has to download new ephemeris data from the fourth satellite, so it takes 15 to 30 seconds to find its position. Your receiver will typically perform a warm start if it has been between three and six hours since you last used it.

Hot start. When you turn your receiver on within a few hours from when it was last used, the almanac and ephemeris data stored in its memory are still valid. In this case, your receiver can find its position in only a few seconds. Ephemeris data remains valid for about three hours. If it has been less than three hours since you last found your position, your receiver will perform a hot start.

When your receiver is downloading ephemeris data, it must receive a complete message from each satellite without interruption. Published acquisition times assume you are standing still with a clear view of the sky. When you are moving, acquisition may take considerably longer. If you momentarily lose the signal as you travel under a bridge or through tree cover, your receiver has to start over. Depending on how often the signals are interrupted, acquisition can take many minutes. Also note that in all cases, the almanac data is assumed to be valid. As indicated earlier, without a valid almanac, it may take more than 12 minutes and as long as an hour to determine your position, although many newer receivers have improvements that reduce this time (see sidebar on facing page).

THE QUEST TO IMPROVE ACQUISITION TIME

The Achilles' heel of GPS has always been how long it takes to find your position when your receiver hasn't been recently used. If it hasn't been turned on in a few days, it could take several minutes, and if it hasn't been turned on in several months, it could take 15 minutes or more. Manufacturers are constantly striving to improve this performance, and while they can't change the basic design of the GPS system, they have continued to improve their receivers. Three recent improvements are particularly noteworthy.

First, manufacturers continue to increase the number of parallel channels in their receivers' electronics. Until recently, 12-channel receivers were the norm. Today, it's not unusual for receivers to have 32 channels or more. Since there can be as many as 32 active GPS satellites at any time, you might think each channel is dedicated to a specific satellite, but this isn't the best way to use all 32 channels. Instead, several channels may be devoted to tracking a single satellite at different frequencies. The satellites are in constant motion either toward or away from you, which causes their signals to undergo slight changes in frequency known as Doppler shifts. The amount of the shift depends on the apparent speed and direction of the satellite at any given moment. By devoting several parallel channels to a single satellite, your receiver can speed acquisition by searching simultaneously over multiple frequencies.

To overcome the delay associated with downloading a full almanac, many receivers now come with a default almanac stored permanently in memory. That way, even if the current almanac gets out-of-date, the receiver can usually still get a position fix without waiting for a new almanac to download. Another improvement is the use of a technology called "Long Term Orbits" to predict satellite ephemeris data up to 7 days in advance. This technology was first developed for GPS-enabled mobile phones (see page 35), where the data is stored on the cellular network and accessed by the phone whenever necessary. A similar technology is now finding its way into dedicated GPS receivers, but a dedicated receiver can't call up a cellular network to get the data. Manufacturers don't publicize how their software actually works, but you can usually identify such receivers because they are advertised as being able to find their positions in less than a minute in all conditions.

GETTING TO KNOW YOUR GPS RECEIVER

If you've recently bought a new GPS receiver, now is a good time to get acquainted with it. Take it out of the box and scan the owner's manual to learn how to do things like load the batteries and turn it on. With some receivers, you have to accept a warning message by pushing the ENTER key before it will find your position. Others begin to acquire satellites immediately after being turned on. Don't be afraid to experiment and push buttons; you can't hurt your receiver by doing so, and you'll quickly become familiar with it.

The first time you take your receiver out of the box, you will probably have to initialize it. In the past, initialization was tedious. The receiver would display a map of the world, and you would have to move a cursor to your approximate location. It could then take many minutes to find your position. Most modern receivers perform an automatic initialization; all you do is go outside to give your receiver a clear view of the sky, turn it on, and wait a few minutes for it to acquire the satellites. When done, it reports that it has found your position and displays your current latitude and longitude.

The next thing to do is learn how to scroll through the various screens, or "pages," of the display. Most GPS receivers work similarly: You push a button typically labeled something like PAGE or NAV (Navigation) to cycle through a series of pages that display information or allow you to perform various tasks. Each time you push the PAGE button, you move to the next page, eventually returning to the first page.

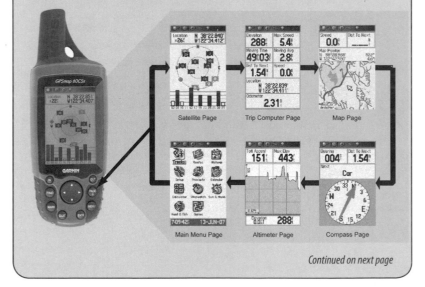

Satellite Page   Trip Computer Page   Map Page

Main Menu Page   Altimeter Page   Compass Page

Continued on next page

You can usually also cycle through the pages in reverse by pushing a button called QUIT or ESC (Escape). Some newer touch screen receivers like the Garmin Oregon and Dakota families, in a somewhat different approach, use an icon-based main screen similar to a high-end mobile phone, which allows you to access any page immediately without having to scroll through each page in succession. The pages themselves, though, are similar to other receivers.

A simple, non-mapping receiver has only a few pages. Mapping receivers add several additional pages. Every receiver typically includes at least the following pages:

SATELLITE: This page shows you all the satellites your receiver is tracking and where they are located in the sky. Some satellite pages also show additional information such as your current latitude and longitude.

COMPASS: This page looks like a compass, but think of it as a heading indicator, not a true magnetic compass. (See page 34.) When you are moving, it orients itself to your direction of travel. When you have initiated a GOTO function, it displays an arrow pointing in the direction of your destination.

MAP: On a mapping receiver, this page displays the map detail. On a non-mapping receiver, it is a blank slate that shows your track and the locations of stored waypoints.

TRIP INFORMATION: This page shows a variety of information about your trip. You can typically customize the page to show such things as your location, speed, distance traveled, distance to destination, elevation, etc.

SETUP or **MAIN MENU** (Garmin receivers): This page is where you customize your receiver for such things as latitude-longitude or UTM coordinates, map datum, north reference, etc. On Magellan and Lowrance receivers, this page is accessed from the menu button.

On each page, you can access additional information by pushing the MENU button. (On grayscale eTrex receivers, this button is a pull-down menu icon at the upper right corner of the screen.) From here, you can customize the appearance of the page or change the displayed data. After you've made the desired changes, push the QUIT or ESC button to return to the main page.

Once you become familiar with the basic operation of your receiver, you will probably want to use the MENU button to make a few changes to the default configuration. (Read your owner's manual to learn how to do this.) Recommended changes include:

Continued on next page

Compass heading: Out of the box, many receivers are configured to display bearings as cardinal points of the compass (north, south, east, west). You will want to change that to the much more useful DEGREES format. In addition, the compass page can often be configured to display additional data. If so, set it up to display BEARING and DISTANCE to your next destination.

Position format: Most receivers come preset to display degrees-decimal minutes, a good default format, but check to make sure that's what is set. Hikers and backpackers may want to change it to UTM.

Map datum: Out of the box it is WGS 84. If you need NAD 27 or some other datum, change it now.

Satellite view: Some receivers, most notably the least expensive members of Garmin's eTrex series, come preprogrammed to display a very simple satellite page of limited usefulness. Change it to the more detailed display showing the locations of the satellites in the sky and the strengths of their signals.

You're now ready to explore the other features of your receiver. The two most important are the MARK and GOTO (sometimes called FIND) functions, described elsewhere in this chapter. If they are not obvious buttons on your receiver, take the time to learn how to access these features now. Other useful buttons include IN and OUT (used to zoom in and out on the map page), and an arrow keypad that allows you to scroll around to different locations on a screen. Some receivers replace the keypad with a multipurpose joystick.

You will likely have questions about your receiver's operation that aren't answered in the owner's manual. If so, check the manufacturer's website for FAQs and other information. If one exists, you may also want to join an online forum that covers your receiver. For Garmin receivers, check the Google group at http://groups.google.com/group/alt.satellite.gps.garmin/topics, and for Magellan, at http://groups.google.com/group/alt.satellite.gps.magellan/topics. DeLorme also hosts a forum for their PN-series receivers and other products at http://forum.delorme.com.

Features of GPS Receivers

Like everything electronic, GPS receiver technology is advancing rapidly. Size, weight, and power consumption drop every year. It's now possible to buy a GPS receiver built into your wristwatch, your mobile phone, your camera, and your handheld two-way radio. Who knows what we'll see in the next few years.

For wilderness navigation, you don't need a lot of receiver horsepower; you'll be more concerned with keeping down size and weight. Of course, if you can afford it, you'll certainly want to consider a receiver with more features, but the minimum feature set you need includes the ability to do the following:

▶ Report your position in latitude and longitude.

▶ Accept different map datums. In North America the absolute minimum includes the two formats known as WGS 84 and NAD 27.

▶ Determine your speed and direction of travel.

▶ Store the locations of numerous points of interest, called waypoints.

▶ Calculate the direction and distance from your current location to any stored waypoint and from one waypoint to another.

The Garmin Rino is a GPS receiver built into a two-way radio.

▶ Plot a "breadcrumb" trail, or track log, of your path as you move around.

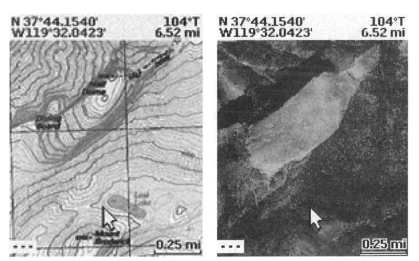

When loaded with the appropriate software, mapping receivers can display detailed topographic maps. The DeLorme PN-40 can display both scanned USGS 7.5-minute topo maps and aerial photographs.

The next chapter covers waypoints and bearings; latitude and longitude, UTM, and map datums are covered in Chapter 4; and track logs are described in Chapter 12.

GPS receivers for outdoor use come in two levels of complexity. Entry-level receivers are inexpensive units that provide all the basic features you need but not much more. Mapping receivers have the ability to display full-featured maps, including towns, rivers, roads, and sometimes topographic features. They typically come factory-loaded with a fairly simple base map of major North American cities and highways. By purchasing additional software, you can load more detailed street or topographic maps (limited only by the receiver's available memory). With the right map, a high-end mapping receiver can even give you turn-by-turn driving directions to any street address you enter, although it will only display text messages, not audible voice commands like those found in a dedicated highway navigation receiver. More expensive receivers may include additional features such as a barometric altimeter and a magnetic compass.

If you're looking to buy a used receiver, you may come across a third type, the so-called intermediate receivers. They include a simple database of towns and other points of interest but can't display detailed maps of roads or highways. A few intermediate receivers are still sold new, but as true mapping receivers have become more affordable, intermediate receivers have fallen from favor.

Outdoor navigation doesn't require a high-end receiver. At minimum, you want one that is small and lightweight, has waterproof construction, and includes the minimum features listed on page 23. If you're only going to use it for outdoor recreation and can't afford to spend a lot of money, a basic, entry-level receiver will do fine. Ignore Internet reviews that disparage low-end products. Modern name-brand receivers work just fine, although there's always a chance you'll eventually outgrow them and long for more features. Extra gadgets like true barometric altimeters or magnetic compasses are fun toys if you can afford them, but hardly essential. That doesn't mean a magnetic compass isn't important—it is. It's just not necessary to have it built into your receiver. In fact, as I'll stress more than once, even if your receiver includes a built-in magnetic compass, my strong advice is that you still carry a separate compass. It's never smart to pin all your navigation hopes on the vagaries of a single, battery-powered electronic instrument, no matter how much you paid for it.

If you also intend to use your receiver for highway navigation, you'll want a more expensive unit with mapping capability. Here you'll have to make a trade-off. Smaller, lighter units have smaller screens that are harder to see while driving. (Be sure your passenger is the one looking at the screen while you're driving!) Larger units with bigger screens are great on the highway but cumbersome on a hike. In my opinion, smaller is better, so I'll take what I get while driving. But you may make a different compromise. You may even want to buy a separate unit designed specifically for highway use or purchase highway navigation software for your mobile phone. These items won't replace your outdoor receiver as they don't have the waypoint and tracking features you'll need in the wilderness, but they are more useful on the highway. The following discussion shows you what to look for in a receiver intended for outdoor use, starting with key GPS features. For detailed information on current models suitable for outdoor navigation, refer to Chapter 15.

Display

Less expensive receivers use black-and-white LCD displays. High-end receivers use color LCD displays optimized for viewing in bright sunlight. Color is an advantage in a mapping receiver that must portray a lot of information at once. In the past, color displays were difficult to read in bright sunlight, so if you're in the market for a used receiver, do your own tests before purchasing one. Most receivers allow you to activate a backlight so you can read the display in dim light. Inexpensive receivers don't need to show a lot of data and can get away with low-resolution displays. Mapping receivers need higher resolution.

Some newer receivers use color touch screens that eliminate the need for physical buttons. Although similar in principle to the touch screens found on some mobile phones, they are not the same. GPS receivers use transreflective TFT screens that extend battery life compared to a typical mobile phone but are not as easy to read in direct sunlight.

Compare the screen resolution of two Garmin receivers. The basic eTrex (left) is a non-mapping receiver with a low-resolution display. The GPSMAP 60CSx is a mapping receiver that needs a high-resolution display. Despite their appearances, these compass displays do not completely eliminate the need for a separate magnetic compass.

Antenna

Your receiver uses one of two types of antennas, either a quadrifilar helix antenna or a patch antenna. Quadrifilar helix antennas are coils of wire beneath a plastic cover that typically extend beyond the main body of the receiver. Sometimes they are detachable, which can be useful in an automobile. In other units, they are solidly attached but stick out from the top of the receiver.

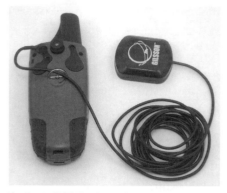

The Garmin GPSMAP 60CSx can be used with a separate external antenna. Note how the antenna cable has been routed under the D-ring to better protect the miniature MCX connector.

Patch antennas look like small, rectangular metal sandwiches. They're easy to build into the main receiver unit, so if yours doesn't have some sort of appendage sticking out of it, it probably uses a patch antenna. Either kind works well if you hold the unit properly. Units with a patch antenna, like the Garmin eTrex series, get best reception when held horizontally. Units with a quadrifilar helix antenna, like the Garmin GPSMAP 60 series, typically should be held vertically, but check your instruction manual for more information.

Some receivers have a connector that allows you to attach an external antenna. While not essential, it can be useful. In a car, it allows you to place the antenna where it has a good view of the sky while keeping the receiver on a dashboard bracket for easy viewing. In the field, you can attach the antenna to your clothing and put the receiver in your pocket. This is great if you want to record a continuous track of your journey, such as when you're mapping out the complete route of a hiking or biking trail. Any receiver placed in your pocket will likely lose satellite reception, so if you don't use an external antenna, you'll need to keep it out where it has a good view of the sky.

Receiver

Inside the unit behind the antenna is the receiver system. All modern units have at least 12 channels so they can track up to 12 satellites simultaneously; some receivers have even more channels, allowing them to get a position fix even faster. Some older models had only one- or two-channel receivers. But they still needed to track four satellites to get a position fix, so they had to sequentially switch between the different satellites. It's the equivalent of a TV couch potato trying to watch four different shows by using his remote control to switch through them in quick succession. Like the couch potato, these older receivers missed some information, so they took a lot longer to get a position fix and were never as accurate as true 12-channel receivers. If you're thinking of buying a used receiver, make sure it has 12 *parallel* channels. Be careful, because some receivers were advertised as being able to "track up to 12 satellites" but could only track two satellites at a time.

Receiver technology, like all electronics, constantly improves. Most new receivers have much improved sensitivity and can lock onto satellites even indoors or under heavy tree cover. If this capability is important to you, look for a product that is advertised as using a high-sensitivity GPS receiver chip.

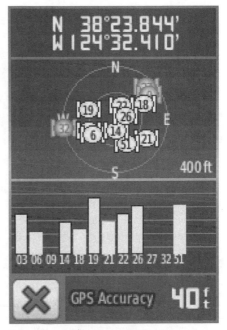

The satellite page (sample from the Garmin Dakota) shows the strength of each signal and the location of each satellite in the sky.

Memory

A mapping receiver's built-in map (known as a base map) doesn't contain a lot of detail. It is typically limited to interstate highways, a few arterial roads, and major cities. If you want to do serious road navigation or view topographic contours, you need to load more detailed maps into its memory. Not just any map will do; the software must be compatible with your receiver. Using a computer, you can then load more detailed maps. The amount of detail is limited by your receiver's memory. With 8 MB you might be limited to the streets of a single city. With 64 MB you could load a significant part of a state. Even with a 64-MB receiver, on a long cross-country trip you might need to bring along a laptop computer to occasionally load new maps.

The trend these days is for receivers to accept external memory cards, which lets you easily swap maps without the need for a computer.

Garmin receivers typically use microSD cards, while Lowrance and Magellan use standard SD cards. Before leaving on your trip, store as many maps as necessary onto memory cards (you may need several cards, depending on the extent of your journey). Then when you need a new map, just swap cards.

Some mapping receivers such as this Lowrance iFinder H20c can accept external memory cards. (Courtesy of Lowrance)

Mapping receivers from most major manufacturers only accept maps from their own proprietary software programs. Each company offers various types of maps covering such things as metropolitan streets, highway points of interest, topographic features, or marine navigation aids and obstructions. Unfortunately, if you also use one of the excellent third-party topographic mapping software programs such as National Geographic's TOPO! or Maptech's Terrain Navigator, you'll be disappointed to learn that while they let you upload waypoints and routes into your receiver, you can't upload the maps themselves.

At present, there are two exceptions to this trend. Magellan lets you load National Geographic's TOPO! maps into their Triton receivers, and Garmin offers a Custom Maps software tool that allows you to create and load custom maps into their Oregon, Dakota, and Colorado receivers (see page 108 for more information).

Computer Port

Many receivers let you transfer data between your receiver and your personal computer. You can send information both ways—download stored waypoints, tracks, and routes from your receiver to your PC, and upload them from your PC to your receiver. You'll need two things to do this: a software program to handle the exchange and a data cable to connect your receiver to the PC. Most software programs have been designed for Windows PCs. Mac support is much harder to find. You can get the software either from the receiver manufacturer or from third parties like National Geographic (www.natgeomaps.com/software.html) or DeLorme (www.delorme.com).

Modern GPS receivers connect to a computer through the USB interface, a fast, efficient way to transfer data. Some receivers still use the old RS-232 serial port—an approach with a couple problems. First, the transfer rate is excruciatingly slow—tolerable if you're only transferring waypoints and track logs, but transferring 24 MB of map data takes more than an hour. Second, serial ports are old technology, and most new PCs don't even come with one. It is possible to use a USB-to-serial converter, but manufacturers caution that not all such converters will work with their receivers. And even if it does work, the transfer speed is limited to that of the serial port. If you're going to transfer much data between a GPS receiver and a computer, look for a receiver with a USB interface.

Power

As receivers continue to get smaller and lighter, their power requirements are also dropping. Not long ago the smallest receivers were powered by four AA cells. Now they use only two AA cells, and some even use AAA cells. A minor trade-off is that battery life is sometimes shorter, although improvements in receiver technology continue to reduce power requirements. With a newer receiver you can expect to get a minimum of 15 to 20 hours out of a set of alkaline or high-capacity nickel-metal hydride (NiMH) batteries. If you're wondering how you'll get through a three-day hike with a receiver that runs for only 15 hours, understand that you shouldn't need to leave it on all the time. Just turn it on for a few minutes whenever you need a position fix or an updated bearing and distance to your destination. With this approach, you should be able to get through even a two-week journey without problems. If you're concerned, you can always pack extra batteries.

It's a little different if you're using your receiver in a car. In this case, you'll probably leave it turned on for extended periods, so you'll want to spend extra money on a cable that lets you plug it into your car's cigarette lighter. If this kind of use is important, make sure to buy a receiver that can operate from an external power source.

Water Resistance

Buy a receiver designed to be waterproof. Even if you don't intend to take it on a lake or river, you don't want it to be damaged by rainfall or an accidental coffee spill. The relevant industry standard is known as IEC 60529 IPX7. Receivers that meet this standard can survive accidental immersion in a meter of water for up to 30 minutes. They are not intended for continuous underwater use, but since GPS signals don't travel underwater, this level of protection isn't necessary. Note that the IEC standard doesn't require that the unit float. Some do, some don't, so if you plan to use it in a kayak or boat, you might want to make sure your chosen unit is designed to float, not plummet to the bottom, if accidentally dropped overboard.

Data Reporting and Analysis

Most GPS receivers designed for outdoor use can give you far more information than you're ever likely to need. The following list is useful in helping you weed out receivers that really aren't intended for wilderness navigation. All of these features will be discussed more fully in later chapters. Here's what to look for:

Position format in latitude and longitude. Most people will never need to use anything else, although inveterate backpackers occasionally swear by the UTM coordinate system. Any good unit will also have a dozen or more other formats that look good on the data sheet but will probably never get used—the West Malayan RTO and the EOV Hungarian Grid are two that come to mind.

Map datum choices that include at least WGS 84 and NAD 27. WGS 84 is the native datum of the GPS system, and NAD 27 is a North American datum used on many older topographic maps. Travelers to the United Kingdom who use local maps will need the datum called "Ordinance Survey GB," while travelers elsewhere in Europe may need the "European Datum 1950." In Japan, the "Tokyo Datum" may be useful. Datums are covered in more detail in Chapter 4. As with position format, most receivers provide dozens of other datums, including such all-time favorites as Liberia 1960 and Ascension Island 1958. Admittedly, a few of these are important if you intend to do much international travel, but mostly they just clutter up the screen and make it harder to find the ones you really need.

A typical GPS receiver can display a wide variety of data about your trip. The TRIP COMPUTER screen of the Garmin Oregon lets you customize the displayed data. Most of this information will only be accurate if you remember to clear memory before starting your trip.

Ability to mark and store waypoints. This feature is one of the two most important ones you'll use. You'll learn more about waypoints in the next chapter. Look for a receiver that can store at least 500 waypoints.

Easily accessible GOTO **(sometimes called** FIND**) function.** This second of the two most important GPS features allows you to find the distance and bearing to your destination. Chapter 3 covers how to use this function. Once upon a time, all self-respecting receivers had dedicated GOTO buttons, but nowadays some of the smaller ones have given this up—you'll have to search for it buried among the various screen displays. High-end receivers often label this a FIND button. With this function, the receiver can tell you not only how to get to way-points, but also, with the right map loaded in memory, how to get to addresses and points of interest.

GPS receivers like this Lowrance iFinder H20c typically offer 100 or more datum choices.

North reference. At minimum, you should be able to select between true north and magnetic north, as discussed in the next chapter.

Compass display. This screen includes the two most important pieces of data you'll normally need: the bearing and distance to your intended destination. Although it's not a substitute for a true magnetic compass, which tells you the direction it's pointing, the compass pointer is still useful. When you're moving, it does a pretty good job of showing you the direction to your destination. When you're stopped, though, it's useless. The compass display tells you only the direction you're moving, not the direction the receiver is pointing. For applications such as geocaching, when you're not likely to get lost, you may be able to get by with this display in place of a magnetic compass. For any serious wilderness navigation, though, you should carry a separate compass. Many receivers allow you to change this display from one that looks like a compass to one that looks like a highway. Stick with the compass display.

Route capability. This tool is useful for guiding you on a multipart hike. It's like an enhanced GOTO function. You specify the waypoints you want to go to and the sequence in which you want to reach them; the route function automates the process of going to each of them in succession. You could, of course, do the same thing manually, but you're less likely to make a mistake if you've entered the information as a route.

Any receiver that offers all of these features will probably offer many others. Some are useful, but most are just niceties. Sunrise, sunset, time of day, and trip odometer, for example, could provide useful information. Glide ratio, velocity made good, and estimated time of arrival are designed for aircraft or marine navigation and don't have much use in the outdoors.

WAAS reception. As described in Chapter 1, WAAS is operated by the Federal Aviation Administration to improve GPS accuracy for aircraft navigation. Using WAAS, it is possible to improve measurement accuracy to better than 3 meters (10 feet).

It sounds great, but because the geosynchronous satellites orbit over the equator, they appear low in the sky to ground-based observers in the U.S. They are often blocked by the surrounding terrain, trees, or buildings, making WAAS marginally useful for outdoor enthusiasts. It was developed for aircraft navigation, and that is where it shines.

Although most GPS receivers for the outdoor market include WAAS capability, it is hardly essential. In fact, it is even possible that WAAS signals could reduce your accuracy if you are outside the U.S. Since all the WAAS ground stations are located in North America, the WAAS correction factors are only valid within this region. But they can still be received even when you are in Mexico or South America. If you have WAAS turned on, your receiver will apply these invalid correction factors, which could worsen your accuracy. It is often better to turn off WAAS—you'll get position fixes faster and consume less battery power.

Limitations of GPS

GPS is so powerful that it's easy to forget it also has limitations. These are especially likely to show up in wilderness navigation. You should understand and know how to deal with them.

Satellite visibility. Since it depends on satellites to operate, your receiver needs a clear view of the sky—at least enough to lock onto four different satellites. If you're in a narrow canyon or surrounded by tall buildings, your receiver probably won't work. Nor will it work indoors. And it might not work under heavy tree cover because the water in tree leaves blocks the satellite signals. In a leafy forest, your receiver will work better in the fall and winter, when the leaves have fallen from the trees. On the other hand, clouds, rain, and snow won't significantly affect your reception. A solid film of water blocks the signals, but water vapor or isolated droplets don't. That's also why you can't use a GPS receiver underwater.

A larger receiver might work better for this application because it will probably have a more sensitive antenna. Some newer receivers use very sensitive, integrated circuits from SiRF Technology or Global

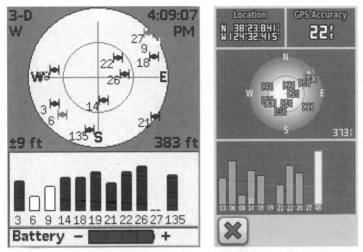

Be sure you know how to tell your receiver is operating in 3D mode. The DeLorme PN-40 (left) explicitly indicates its state in the upper left corner of the display. On the Garmin Oregon (right) you must observe the satellite strength indicators to confirm at least four satellites are being tracked.

Locate that work much better indoors and under heavy tree cover. But even the best receiver won't work in all cases. The satellite page on your receiver will help you see how good your reception is. Check it occasionally. With practice, you'll be able to predict when you're about to lose coverage.

Requires at least four satellites. For best accuracy, your receiver must be locked onto at least four satellites. This is called the "3D operating mode" because it accurately finds your position in all three dimensions. But sometimes terrain or tree cover blocks signals, and your receiver won't lock onto four satellites. If it can lock onto three satellites, it will operate in what's known as "2D mode." It will still calculate a position, but it won't be as accurate. In 2D mode, your receiver compensates for the missing satellite by estimating your elevation. However, the only elevation it knows is the last one it measured, so that's what it uses. But if you've changed your position since then, your elevation could have changed by hundreds or thousands of feet, and the calculated position can be off by a mile or more. If you know your current elevation, you can possibly improve accuracy by manually entering it. But in general, 2D navigation is nearly useless and even dangerous for wilderness navigation—never depend on it.

If 2D mode is nearly useless, why do manufacturers provide it? It does work on the ocean, where the elevation is constant, but it's almost never necessary there because you always have a clear view to the horizon and can easily lock onto four satellites. 2D mode is a holdover from the early days of GPS, before all 24 satellites were deployed. There's little need for it today.

Manufacturers don't do a very good job of explaining this limitation. Instruction manuals often refer to the fact that "elevation is not being computed," but they don't explain the impact on accuracy. Some newer units don't even explicitly tell you whether they're operating in 2D or 3D mode. You have to figure it out for yourself by looking at the satellite page to see how many satellites are being tracked. Make sure you know how to confirm your receiver is operating in 3D mode before you rely on its data.

Inaccurate elevation. GPS was designed to find your position anywhere on earth, but it was not designed to accurately measure your elevation. All GPS receivers give you an elevation readout, but you can't depend on it. Its accuracy depends on the geometry of the satellites in the sky. When they are well spread out, it can be reasonably accurate, but when they are closely grouped, it can be off by a thousand feet or more. If you want accurate elevations, use a calibrated barometric altimeter (some more expensive units come with one built in).

It's not a compass. Remember that a GPS receiver is not a compass. Even though every receiver has a screen that looks like a compass display, this screen only tells you what direction you're moving, not what direction the unit is pointed. So it is really a heading indicator, not a true compass. To navigate safely in the wilderness, even with a GPS unit, you must be able to accurately determine direction. Always carry a separate magnetic compass.

Today, some receivers include a built-in magnetic compass. Known as an electronic fluxgate compass, it is accurate to within about 5 degrees. But when turned on, it rapidly uses up batteries. While a receiver with a built-in magnetic compass can cost more than $50 more than a similar one without it, you can buy a quality magnetic compass for less than $20. If you have a unit with a built-in compass, go ahead and use it, but still carry a separate compass. That way, if your receiver gets damaged or its batteries fail, you're not completely helpless.

GPS-Enabled Mobile Phones

Now that GPS technology has become ubiquitous in the new generation of smart mobile phones ("smartphones"), a logical question is whether such phones are a suitable replacement for a standalone GPS receiver. If you primarily use GPS for highway navigation and don't mind looking at a small screen the answer might be *yes*, but at least today, the answer for the outdoor navigator is *probably not*.

This response might surprise some people. "My iPhone has a true GPS receiver just like a Garmin, so why should I need anything else?" The answer comes from design tradeoffs made by mobile phone designers. One tradeoff is that smartphones such as the iPhone or Blackberry are not as rugged as outdoor receivers from such manufacturers as Garmin, DeLorme, Lowrance, or Magellan. While dedicated GPS receivers from any of these manufacturers are waterproof to the IPX7 standard, most smartphone warranties are voided if the unit gets wet.

Another issue is that of battery life. Smartphones typically aren't optimized for continuous GPS use. Leave the GPS function turned on continuously and you may discover your battery is dead after only two or three hours.

A third issue relates to receiver sensitivity. A dedicated GPS receiver is optimized for use in the outdoors, while a smartphone optimizes its GPS performance around cost. One difference is that a dedicated receiver typically includes a much better antenna than a smartphone, and it will perform better in difficult conditions such as areas of heavy tree cover.

Finally, keep in mind that a GPS-enabled smartphone might not always find your position when you are far out in the wilderness. The issue comes from their use of a technology known as Assisted GPS or simply A-GPS. This clever technology allows the GPS in your mobile phone to obtain a position fix very rapidly by using information it gets from the cellular network. As we learned earlier in this chapter, one limitation on how fast a dedicated GPS receiver can obtain a position fix is the length of time it takes to download almanac and ephemeris information from the satellites—a minute or more for ephemeris data and more than 12 minutes for a new almanac. Mobile phone designers realized they didn't need to depend on the satellites to collect this information. Because the receiver is also a phone, it can call up and get the data from the cellular network nearly instantaneously—something a dedicated GPS receiver can't do.

This works fine as long as the smartphone is within the coverage area of a cellular network. If not, it won't always work. If the smartphone already has valid almanac and ephemeris data because its GPS function was recently turned on while inside a coverage area, everything works fine. But if not, the smartphone will try to access the network to get it. But without network connectivity, it will be unsuccessful. It then reverts to acquiring the data directly from the satellites, which takes much longer. Some GPS software apps won't tolerate this delay, and others don't even work unless they are connected to a network.

If your activities are limited to geocaching in a local park, a GPS-enabled smartphone may be all you need. If you intend to spend much time outside a cellular network coverage area or if you need a more rugged, waterproof receiver, stick with one designed specifically for outdoor use.

Navigation Using
Waypoints and Bearings

The simplest thing you can do with your GPS receiver is find your way back to a place you've been to before—a favorite campsite, fishing spot, or even your car in the mall parking lot. You can perform this basic navigation without knowing anything about such things as latitude, longitude, position formats, UTM, or map datums. You just need to know how to store your current location as a GPS waypoint and how to return to it using your receiver's GOTO (sometimes called FIND) function. You'll also need to know how to navigate by following a bearing. So this chapter covers waypoints, bearings, and your receiver's MARK and GOTO functions.

Consider an example: Suppose you intend to spend the afternoon exploring unfamiliar territory. Maybe you're a hunter going where the game takes you or a photographer looking for that great shot. Either way, you don't have a planned itinerary and might not follow established trails. You need to make sure you can get back to the trailhead before dark. So here's what to do: Store the location of the trailhead as a GPS waypoint before you start out. When you're ready to return, let your receiver show you how to get back to it. If you know how to follow a bearing, you should have little trouble getting back.

Waypoints

Waypoints (sometimes called landmarks or points of interest) are one of the most basic GPS concepts. Think of it as something like a street address. Suppose you live at 123 Center Street, Anytown, USA. Your address is simply a way to describe exactly where you live. It's how the post office knows where to deliver your mail, how the pizza parlor knows where to deliver that delicious dinner you ordered.

Waypoints are the GPS equivalent of street addresses, but of course they aren't limited to streets. The Global Positioning System uses a mathematical model of the entire earth to describe the coordinates of any point on it. Most often, this will be in the form of latitude and longitude, but your GPS receiver can use many other formats as well. In fact, regardless of what format you specify, your receiver always stores the information in its own internal format referenced to the center of the earth. It applies complicated mathematical formulas to convert this internal format into something more useful to humans, like latitude and longitude or UTM coordinates.

Using waypoints, it's possible to do things like record the position of a tree in your front yard separately from another tree in your backyard. But remember, GPS accuracy is only about 25 feet, so don't depend on it to determine positions better than that. You can't use your consumer GPS receiver to accurately survey your property lines, for example, although it is possible to do so with certain very expensive commercial units and additional computer software.

A typical consumer GPS receiver can store 500 or more locations in its waypoint database. You can store them in several ways. The simplest, though not always the easiest, is to go to the desired location and push the buttons that tell your receiver to store your current location in memory. That's what is covered in this chapter. Chapter 4 shows you how to enter the latitude and longitude or UTM coordinates of a location without actually having to go there. Chapter 7 teaches you how to use a computer and mapping software to upload waypoints without having to arduously key in the numbers.

Once you've stored a waypoint, you can go wherever you want, and your GPS receiver can always show you how far away and what direction that waypoint is from your current position. Then you simply head in the right direction until you get back to it. But to do this, you need to know a bit about direction-finding in the wilderness.

Directions and Bearings

We are all familiar with how to describe directions in terms of the four cardinal points of the compass—north, south, east, and west. Intermediate directions include northeast, southeast, southwest, and northwest. Many GPS receivers even let you display bearings in this format. But it's not very precise.

A better way is based on the Greek system of dividing the full circle into 360°. North is defined as the reference direction at 0°. Going clockwise around the circle, east is at 90°, south at 180°, and west at 270°.

With this approach, you can describe a direction very accurately. A mountain in the distance that's directly east of you is said to be at a bearing of 90°. Another peak that's directly southwest is at a bearing of 225°. With care, using a good magnetic compass, you can measure the bearing to a distant object to an accuracy of about 2 degrees. You'll learn how to do that later in this chapter.

In GPS terminology, the term *bearing* is used to describe the direction between your current position and your desired destination. In contrast, the term *heading* describes the direction you are traveling. (Purists use *azimuth* instead of bearing, and *track* instead of heading, but *bearing* and *heading* have become dominant in the GPS world.) If you're moving directly

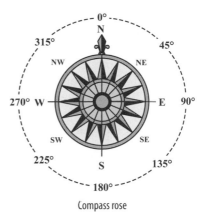

Compass rose

toward your destination, then your heading and your bearing are the same. If not, they are different. Often, you can't head directly along your desired bearing, as when you're navigating around an obstacle such as a mountain.

You can set up your GPS receiver to display either value on its screen (see the figure on page 25). Just make sure you understand the difference between the two terms, and that you use bearing, not heading, to guide you to your destination. When set to display numeric bearings, your GPS receiver can give you a bearing readout to a resolution of 1

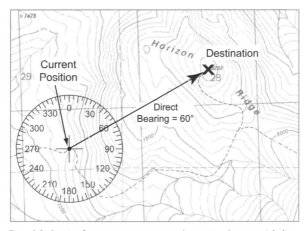

To read the bearing from your position to your destination, draw a straight line between the two points and center a protractor over your current position with 0° oriented due north. Read the bearing where the line intersects the edge of the protractor.

degree. This is more than sufficient for outdoor navigation, where you'll rarely be able to follow a bearing to an accuracy of better than 5 degrees anyway.

Remember that the bearing to an object is a relative, not an absolute number—it depends on where you are. If you're in San Francisco, for example, the bearing to Denver is about due east, or 90°. But if you're in Washington, D.C., Denver is about due west, or 270°. The bearing between you and a target object changes as you move around. Someone standing in a different spot will measure a different bearing to the same object. If the two of you are close together and the object is far away, the difference won't be much, but it's something to keep in mind.

QUADRANT BEARINGS

GPS bearings are measured clockwise from 0° to 360° starting from north. But if you've ever studied a property map prepared by a land surveyor, you've probably come across bearings with strange notations like N30°W or S87°E. These are known as *quadrant bearings*, used by such professionals as surveyors, geologists, and foresters. A quadrant bearing is conceptually similar to a GPS bearing (sometimes called an *azimuth bearing*). The circle is still divided into 360 degrees, but instead of referencing all bearings to north, it is segmented into four independent quadrants. The two quadrants in the upper half circle reference their bearings to north, while the two quadrants in the lower half circle reference their bearings to south.

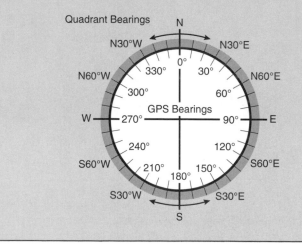

Once you understand the concept of bearings, you can find the bearing from your present position to any destination. Here's how: Using a ruler, draw a straight line on the map connecting your current position with your destination. Now take a protractor (those circular plastic things with numbers on them that you haven't used since grade school) and center it over your current position. Orient it so that 0° points straight north. The bearing to your destination is where the line you drew intersects the edge of the protractor. Check the illustration on page 39 to see how this works. Once you understand it, you're ready to learn how to navigate.

Here's how it works. In the upper half circle, north is at 0°, just as with GPS bearings. As you move either clockwise or counterclockwise from north, the quadrant bearing increases until it reaches 90° at east and west. For example, the bearing for northeast is written as N45°E, which can be thought of as "45 degrees east of north." In the lower half circle, the bearing of 0° is defined as south. Again, as you move clockwise or counterclockwise from there, the quadrant bearing increases to 90° at both east and west. The direction southwest, for example, is written as S45°W. A quadrant bearing can never have a number greater than 90°, and north, south, east, and west are written simply as N, S, E, and W, without a number.

Study the figure to get a better idea of the relationship between quadrant bearings and GPS bearings. For example, a GPS bearing of 120° equates to a quadrant bearing of S60°E because 120° is 60 degrees east of south. Similarly, a quadrant bearing of N30°W equates to a GPS bearing of 330° because that is the direction 30 degrees west of north.

Most consumer GPS receivers can't display quadrant bearings, but if you want to use your receiver to do a rough property survey from a professional surveyor's map, you should understand how to convert quadrant bearings to azimuth bearings. Also note that land surveyors often measure bearings to fractions of a degree, so a bearing of S87°35′52″E is simply a quadrant bearing reported to a resolution of one second of arc.

Simple GPS Navigation

Waypoints and bearings are fundamental to the concept of GPS navigation. To see why, let's go back to our example. Recall that you plan to spend the afternoon exploring unfamiliar territory and want to make sure you can get back to the trailhead before dark. So you need to store the location of the trailhead as a GPS waypoint, which you can do pretty easily when you're standing at the trailhead. You don't need to know anything about latitude or longitude. Just turn on your receiver, wait for it to find its position, and then push the buttons to store that location in memory. This process is known as marking a waypoint.

Every receiver does this a little differently. Some have a dedicated MARK button; push it and it brings up the waypoint screen. Here you can do things like give the waypoint a name or assign it a symbol before you store it. Other receivers don't have a dedicated button; you must select the MARK feature located on one of the menu pages. Such receivers usually have a shortcut way to mark a waypoint, such as by holding down the ENTER key for a couple of seconds. You'll need to read your instruction manual for specific details.

By default, your receiver identifies the waypoint by assigning it a number. After a day of hiking, though, how likely are you to remember you car is at waypoint number 743? You'll be more likely to remember it if you give it a better name. Older receivers often limit you to six alphanumeric characters, although newer units usually allow more. Again, check your manual to see how to enter waypoint names for your unit.

Regardless of which receiver you own, entering a waypoint name is usually a cumbersome process involving lots of button-pushing. You'll

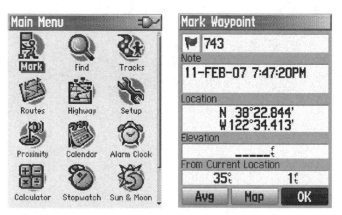

On the Garmin eTrex Venture Cx, you access the MARK WAYPOINT screen from the MAIN MENU. You can also reach it by holding down the Thumb Stick for two seconds.

need quite a bit of practice before you feel comfortable doing it. In Chapter 7, you'll see how to use a computer to make the job easier.

When storing waypoints, check a couple settings. First, make sure your receiver is operating in 3D mode, not 2D mode. Many receivers have an explicit 2D-3D indicator, but if yours doesn't, you might need to check the satellite page to verify it is tracking at least four satellites. Or check the value your receiver reports for its Estimated Position Error (sometimes labeled "EPE" or "Accuracy"). If it's in the neighborhood of 20 to 30 feet or less, you're OK.

One more caution: Don't use the same name as a waypoint already stored in memory. Most receivers won't erase the existing waypoint, but they don't always make it obvious that they haven't stored the new one. This problem most often comes up if you use the same name repeatedly, such as "CAR," to indicate the location of your car. Check the list of existing waypoints and delete any previous waypoint with the same name. Many Garmin receivers have a nifty feature called REPOSITION HERE. You call up an existing waypoint, and with one touch, you can move that waypoint to your current location.

Once you've stored the location of the trailhead, you are ready to go out and explore. Turn off your receiver and put it in your pocket. There's no reason to keep it turned on all the time unless you really want to record a complete track log of your journey as described in Chapter 13. Leaving it on quickly uses up your batteries, and you probably won't get very good reception anyway if it's packed away in a pocket or backpack.

GOTO *Function*

After a few hours of exploration, you're ready to return to the trailhead. Now it's time to turn on your receiver and use another important GPS feature, the GOTO function. With this feature, you tell your receiver which waypoint you want to go to, and it automatically calculates the bearing and distance to it. Then you just follow the indicated bearing until you reach the waypoint. (More on following bearings in a moment.)

Again, you need to read your instruction manual to learn how to use your receiver's GOTO function. Some receivers have a dedicated GOTO button: You simply push the button and choose your desired waypoint. With other units, you first have to select the desired waypoint from a waypoint database, either by spelling it or choosing from a list of nearby or recently visited waypoints. When it is displayed, one of the options you can select is GOTO.

On mapping receivers, the GOTO button is often replaced by a FIND button (called WHERE TO? on the Garmin Oregon and Dakota receivers), which allows you to select from a variety of choices that can include waypoints, street addresses, cities, and other points of interest. After choosing WAYPOINTS and selecting the desired waypoint, you then choose GOTO. If your receiver can do turn-by-turn highway navigation, you will have to decide between FOLLOW ROAD or OFF ROAD. Use OFF ROAD for outdoor navigation. It shows you the direct bearing and distance to the selected waypoint. The FOLLOW ROAD choice is what to use when you are driving (covered in Chapter 14).

It's important to realize that when navigating in the outdoors, your receiver will only show you the straight-line direction and distance to your destination. It won't guide you along the path of a meandering trail or river. The section "Commonsense Navigation: Following a Bearing" on page 54 describes how to follow a GPS bearing over real terrain to reach your destination.

Once you've initiated the GOTO function, you should see the bearing and distance

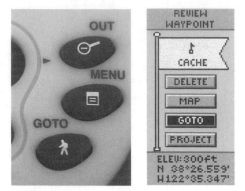

The GOTO function is an essential feature. Know how to use it. The Magellan eXplorist 200 (left) has a dedicated GOTO button. On the Garmin eTrex (right) it is a selection on the WAYPOINT screen.

Mapping receivers such as this GPSMAP 60CSx often replace the GOTO button with a FIND button, allowing you to find not only waypoints but also cities, street addresses, and other points of interest.

The compass page shows you the distance and bearing to a selected waypoint. This is the display from the DeLorme PN-40.

to the selected waypoint, although you might have to scroll through various pages to find the information. Usually, it will at least show up on the compass page, although with some receivers you have to make sure you have configured the display to show a bearing rather than some dubious piece of information like "glide ratio" or "estimated time en route." Once again, check your unit's instruction manual.

OK, that's great. Now you know the bearing and distance to your destination. But how do you know which direction to hike? For that, you need to know how to use a compass to find and follow a bearing.

NAVIGATION PRACTICE

If you have a GPS receiver, now is a good time to practice what you've just learned about using the MARK and GOTO functions.

1. Step outside your house so you have a clear view of the sky, then turn on your GPS receiver. Wait for it to lock on to the satellites and obtain a position fix. (If this is the first time you've turned it on, you might need to perform an initialization. You'll need to read your instruction manual to learn how to do this.) You should see a display showing the latitude and longitude of your current position (you may have to scroll through several pages to find it).

2. Store this location as a GPS waypoint. If your receiver has a MARK button, simply push the button to call up the MARK WAYPOINT screen. If your receiver doesn't have a MARK button, it will probably have a menu page that offers several options, one of which is MARK. (You may have to read your receiver's instruction manual to learn where it is.)

    Once the MARK WAYPOINT screen is displayed, you are ready to save your position as a waypoint. But before doing so, change the name of the waypoint by highlighting the waypoint name and manually entering the word "HOME". Read the instruction manual if you are not sure how to do this. Once you have renamed it, save the waypoint by selecting the SAVE or OK option. You may want to check the waypoint database to make sure it has been saved.

3. Now take a short walk to the end of the block. After you've gotten a few hundred feet from your home, you are ready to find your way back by activating the GOTO function. If your receiver has a GOTO or FIND button, use it to select the waypoint called HOME. If not, call up your receiver's waypoint database and select the waypoint called HOME. (Again, if you're not sure how to do this, review the instruction manual.) One of the choices on the screen should now be GOTO. Select it, and you should be rewarded with a display showing the bearing and distance back to HOME.

Using a Magnetic Compass

While you can often use your GPS receiver's compass page to follow a bearing in the field, you should also understand how to use a magnetic compass. For any serious navigation you *must* carry a separate compass. Let's take a few minutes to understand compasses and how to use them.

Compasses come in many flavors, from dime-store novelties to precision instruments costing many hundreds of dollars. Geologists and foresters swear by the Brunton Pocket Transit, a survey-grade compass that not only finds direction but also can be used to measure angles, height, and slope. It works great in the outdoors, but it's heavy, inconvenient, and pricey. You can get by with something much simpler and less expensive.

The Brunton is an example of a sighting compass, a class that also includes various military-type instruments. They are designed to read bearings to a precision of a degree or less, which can come in handy if you're trying to direct an air strike onto an enemy stronghold while avoiding friendly troops nearby. But it's overkill for wilderness navigators who usually aren't able to follow a bearing to better than 5 degrees anyway.

The best choice for recreational outdoor use is a type called the baseplate compass. (You'll sometimes hear it described as an orienteering compass.) Conveniently, you can get a good baseplate compass for less than $20, and even

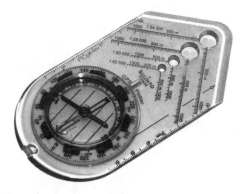

The baseplate compass is the best choice for general outdoor use. On this Suunto GPS Plotter, the entire end of the baseplate is shaped like an arrow, making it easy to determine the direction of travel.

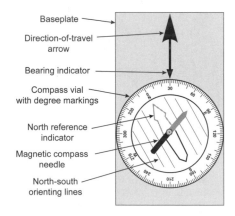

Components of a baseplate compass

the top-of-the-line units rarely cost more than $50. Popular manufacturers include Brunton, Silva, and Suunto.

If wilderness navigation only consisted of knowing which way was north, then just about any compass would do. But in reality, navigation involves two very important steps: First you must determine the bearing from your present location to your destination. Then you have to decide what direction that is in real life. The advantage of a baseplate compass is it can help you in each of these situations. It will also help on those occasions in the field when you want to read the bearing from your current position to an object like a mountain or radio tower in the distance.

Study a baseplate compass and you'll see it has three parts: the baseplate, a compass vial, and a magnetic needle. The cylindrical compass vial contains the all-important magnetic compass needle. The vial is filled with liquid and has degree markings from 0 to 360 on its perimeter. The liquid damps the motion of the needle so it quickly stabilizes its position. (Compare this to cheap compasses in which the needle gyrates wildly at the slightest motion, and you'll appreciate the improvement.) The vial is designed so you can rotate it by hand, but with enough friction so that once positioned it stays put. Look through the vial to its bottom and you can see what looks like the outline of a compass needle pointing to the 0° indicator (the north reference indicator) on the perimeter of the vial, whose use I'll explain in a minute.

Now let's look at the baseplate. The most important thing on it is a direction-of-travel arrow. On most compasses, the arrow is printed along the center of the baseplate, pointing away from the vial, but sometimes the end of the compass itself is shaped like an arrow. The opposite end of the arrow butts up against the compass vial at what is called a bearing indicator. This is what you use to find the direction to your destination. The baseplate also has at least one straight edge you can use to read bearings on a map.

Some compasses include a sighting mirror, which makes it easier to take accurate bearings in the field. When you tilt the mirror at about a

A sighting mirror makes it easier to take accurate bearings in the field. An added benefit is that when the cover is opened all the way, it becomes a long straightedge for measuring bearings on a map.

45-degree angle and hold the compass at eye level, you can look at both the compass vial and the object whose bearing you want. It's nice but not essential.

True vs. Magnetic North

Navigating with a compass would be easier if its magnetic needle always pointed to the North Pole, but it doesn't. For various complicated magnetohydrodynamic reasons, the earth's magnetic field isn't exactly aligned with its axis of rotation; a magnetic compass doesn't point to the true North Pole but rather to a location in northern Canada called magnetic north. The difference between these two directions, which varies depending on where you are on the planet, is known as magnetic declination (called magnetic variation by mariners).

Most maps are referenced to true north, not magnetic north. In the U.S., if you are in the Midwest, it doesn't much matter because the two are nearly the same. The agonic line, or line of zero declination, runs from northern Minnesota to southern Mississippi. But as you move toward either coast, you'll see more difference. As you move west, your compass points too far east. As you move east, it points too far west.

Declination is measured in degrees, and you must specify whether it is east or west. East declination occurs whenever the magnetic needle points too far east; west declination occurs when it points too far west. In the continental U.S., declination ranges from about 20° east to 20°

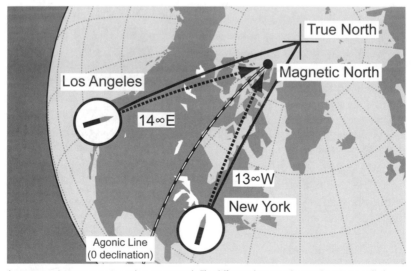

A compass points to magnetic north, not true north. The difference between the two directions is called *magnetic declination*.

west. In Los Angeles, it's about 14° east. In New York City, it's about 13° west. In Alaska it's even worse, exceeding 35° in some areas.

What does this mean? Let's say you're near San Francisco, with a declination of about 15° east. If your GPS receiver is set to give you a bearing referenced to true north (a "true bearing") but your compass is set

A good compass allows you to compensate for magnetic declination. On the left, the compass is set for zero declination. On the right it is set for 15° east declination. Notice how the north reference indicator no longer points to 0°. On this Suunto compass you set declination from the underside of the compass by turning the adjustment screw visible in the upper left portion of the black ring.

to magnetic north (a "magnetic bearing"), you will think you're going in the right direction when you are really headed 15° too far east. Walk only 4 miles in this direction, and you'll have deviated a full mile from your intended path.

The same problem occurs when working with a map. If you measure a bearing from a map and then use a magnetic compass to guide you in the wilderness, you have to compensate for declination.

Most books at this point admonish you to memorize the mathematics used to convert true to magnetic bearings and back, with dubious mnemonics, such as "East is least, west is best." But I'm not going to do that. (If you want to know how to do the math, read the sidebar on page 50.) My advice is to avoid the whole issue by buying a compass with adjustable declination and setting it to the local declination. That way, you don't have to worry about the difference.

Here's how it works: Remember that the north reference indicator on a compass vial normally points to the 0° marking on its perimeter. When you center the magnetic needle inside the indicator, your compass is oriented so that 0° points to magnetic north. But you'd really like 0° to point to true north. Some compasses allow you to adjust the north reference indicator to compensate for declination. Such a compass has a separate declination scale calibrated in degrees east and west, and it allows you to change where the north reference indicator points. For example, to set your compass for 15° east declination, adjust the north reference indicator to point to 15E on the declination scale. Conversely, if you want to set it for 15° west declination, adjust the indicator to 15W on the declination scale. Some compasses provide a little screwdriver on a lanyard you can use to make the adjustment. With others, you do it by hand without any tools. Either way, once it's set, you don't have to worry about doing mental math after an exhausting 10-hour hike.

There's still the little matter of knowing the declination for your location. One way to find out is to check a recent topo map of the area. Magnetic declination is almost always indicated on a topo map, either graphically or in text. Or you can find it from the National Oceanic and Atmospheric Administration (NOAA) magnetic declination website, www.ngdc.noaa.gov/geomag models/Declination.jsp, by entering the zip code or latitude and longitude of the desired location. You can even look it up

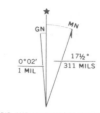

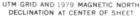

UTM GRID AND 1979 MAGNETIC NORTH
DECLINATION AT CENTER OF SHEET

Declination is always shown on a topographic map. On USGS maps, the star indicates true north, MN indicates magnetic north, and GN indicates grid north, used only in the UTM system. Don't depend on the drawn angle to accurately represent the true declination angle.

CORRECTING FOR MAGNETIC DECLINATION

First, let me point out you shouldn't need to read this. As long as you adopt one of two sensible approaches to GPS navigation, you should never need to do mental arithmetic to correct for declination. My recommendation is to buy a magnetic compass with adjustable declination, set it to the local declination, and set your GPS receiver to display true bearings. Alternatively, you can buy an inexpensive magnetic compass without adjustable declination and set your GPS receiver to display magnetic bearings. Either way, as long as your compass and your GPS receiver are aligned, you don't have to worry about declination.

If you still want to know how to do the math, read on. The situation I describe assumes you are using an inexpensive compass without a declination adjustment, and you have set your GPS receiver to read true bearings.

The rules are simple, if you can remember them. To convert the true bearing reported by your GPS receiver into a magnetic bearing, do the following:

▶ If your magnetic declination is east, subtract declination.

▶ If your magnetic declination is west, add declination.

This is the origin of the mnemonic "East is least, west is best." East being "least" means you subtract declination; and with a little stretch of your imagination, you can say that west being "best" means you add declination.

on your GPS receiver. Go to the SETUP (sometimes called SYSTEM) page and select the feature called "NORTH REFERENCE." Normally, it should be set to true north. But if you change the setting to MAGNETIC (sometimes called AUTO), it will show the declination of your current position to the nearest degree. Make sure you set it back to TRUE north when you are finished.

In the continental U.S., magnetic declination changes only gradually as you change your position. You should easily be able to move 100 miles or more before it's different enough to worry about resetting your compass.

Magnetic declination varies over time. Over the last hundred years, the magnetic pole has moved nearly 900 miles north. In some areas, this has caused a change of more than a degree of declination every 10 years. So check the publication date of any map you use. If it's more than 10 years old, its declination information could be out-of-date. The information on the NOAA website is always current.

Let's take an example: Suppose you are in southern Utah, where the magnetic declination is 13° east. Your GPS receiver tells you your destination waypoint lies at a true bearing of 155°. To convert this to a magnetic bearing, subtract 13° to get a magnetic bearing of 142°.

Now suppose you are in Vermont, where the magnetic declination is 15° west. In this case, you have to add 15°. If your GPS receiver reports a true bearing of 155° then the magnetic bearing is 170°.

If this isn't complicated enough, it gets worse. Let's suppose you're out in the wilderness and see an interesting mountain peak in the distance. To identify it on the map, take a compass reading to measure its bearing. Thanks to your GPS receiver, you know exactly where you are on the map. Draw a line on the map at the correct bearing angle from your current location to see which peak it intersects. Simple enough, right?

Well, if you don't have a compass with adjustable declination, you'll be reading a magnetic bearing. But the map is aligned with true north, so you have to correct the bearing before you plot the line on the map. In this case, though, the situation is reversed. If your declination is east, you have to add declination to the compass reading to get a true bearing. If it's west, you have to subtract. It's enough to make seasoned hikers want to do all their hiking in the Midwest, where declination is close enough to zero that you don't have to worry about it.

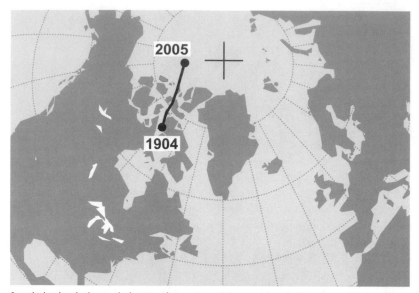

Over the last hundred years, the location of magnetic north has moved nearly 900 miles northwest.

NAVIGATING BY MAGNETIC BEARINGS

This book strongly advocates the use of true bearings when navigating in the outdoors, and the use of a magnetic compass that has been adjusted for the local declination. That way, it's easy to switch between bearings read from a paper map and those shown by your GPS receiver—especially important if you are a serious hiker or backpacker. But sometimes you may want to use magnetic bearings. If you are traveling over long distances where declination changes significantly, it can be problematic to remember to constantly adjust it. That's why aircraft and ships navigate by magnetic bearings. Some search-and-rescue agencies also use magnetic bearings (although not all; if you are part of a SAR team coordinating a search with another agency, make sure you know what they use). And if you only have a simple compass without a declination adjustment, it is easier to use magnetic bearings.

If you choose to navigate by magnetic bearings, set your receiver to display bearings referenced to magnetic north. You can then use a simple compass and not worry about declination adjustments. The techniques described in this chapter for following a bearing work just as well with magnetic bearings as true bearings. But if you choose this approach, you must remember to correct for declination if you ever use your compass to read bearings from a map.

Don't forget to check the north reference setting in your receiver. There are usually several choices: TRUE bearings are referenced to true north. MAGNETIC (sometimes called AUTO) bearings are referenced to magnetic north. Your receiver uses a table stored in memory to compute magnetic declination; after many years, it will become out-of-date. A third choice on some receivers (labeled USER) allows you to manually set declination. (Other choices can include such little-used favorites as GRID, MILITARY TRUE, or MILITARY MAGNETIC. As a civilian wilderness navigator, you will probably never need to worry about these.)

Finding a Bearing in the Field

Now that you have adjusted your compass for your local declination, let's get back to our earlier example: You've been out in the wilderness for the afternoon and now you are ready to go back to the trailhead. You've turned on your GPS receiver and told it to go to the trailhead waypoint, which you've named something like "START." Suppose your receiver says it's 1.5 miles away at a bearing of 135°. That's great, but you still need to know what direction that is in real life.

Here's how to use a baseplate compass to find out: Rotate the compass vial so that 135° is aligned with the bearing indicator. Then hold the compass at waist level so its direction-of-travel arrow is pointing directly away from you. Now you need to orient the compass so that 0° on the vial is pointing directly north. When that happens, you know your direction-of-travel arrow is pointing to a bearing of 135°. To do this, rotate your entire body until the compass needle is boxed inside the north reference indicator on the base of the vial. Make sure you get the correct end of the needle lined up with the correct end of the north reference indicator. Otherwise, you'll head exactly opposite of your intended direction. Usually, you do this by lining up the red end of the arrow with the red end of the indicator. Check out the photo to get a better idea of the process. Once you've got the

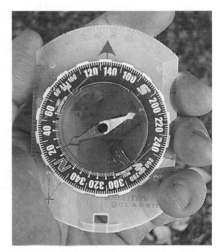

To find a bearing in the field, set the compass vial so the desired bearing aligns with the bearing indicator. Then rotate your body to box the magnetic needle in the north reference indicator. The direction-of-travel indicator now points in the desired direction. Note this compass has been adjusted for 16° east declination.

needle aligned inside the indicator, the direction-of-travel arrow points in the direction of 135°. Head in that direction for 1.5 miles, and you'll be at your car.

One word of caution when using a magnetic compass: It can be affected by nearby metal objects. Vehicles, metal signposts, and belt buckles are common offenders. Even the batteries in your GPS receiver can have an effect. Take off your backpack and stay away from iron or steel objects when taking a compass reading.

Commonsense Navigation: Following a Bearing

Your GPS receiver can only show you the straight-line direction to your destination, not how to navigate around obstacles such as mountains, rivers, or forests. You are rarely able to follow a straight line in the wilderness, although something about GPS always seems to make people want to try. I can't tell you how many times I've watched otherwise sensible people, eyes glued to their receiver, go tramping through dense underbrush, poison oak, and hazardous terrain because, as they explain, "That's the direction my GPS told me to go." Not only is this potentially dangerous, it's a good way to harm a delicate natural environment. Ninety percent of the time, you can get to your destination primarily by following established trails. Most of the rest of the time, a little reconnaissance or advance planning will show you the most sensible route.

The best way to navigate with GPS is to do it the same way you would in the more traditional map-and-compass approach. Use your receiver to find the distance and bearing to your destination, then use your compass to see what direction that is. Look in that direction and pick a distant object like a large tree, mountain peak, or telephone pole you can use as a reference point. Then turn off your receiv-

When following a bearing, look for a feature such as a distant mountain peak in the desired direction. Then put your GPS receiver away and keep the feature in sight as you hike. Take the most logical route toward it rather than blindly following a straight line across difficult terrain. Use your GPS receiver to update the bearing to your destination occasionally, and select a new feature in the distance when necessary.

er and put it away. Use your eyes and brain to find the best route to get to that object. Go around obstacles, not over the top of them. If you lose sight of your goal, pull out your receiver to get an updated bearing, then put it away. When you reach the first reference object, use your receiver to find the new bearing to your destination. Then pick out a new object in the distance and repeat the process. Keep it up until your get to your goal.

One of the most common mistakes made by novices is thinking the bearing they measured at the start of the hike is the same one they should use for the entire hike. They don't realize that unless you are moving directly toward your destination, the bearing to it will change as you move. Fortunately, with GPS, that's not a problem. Just remember to occasionally turn on your receiver and get a current update of the bearing and distance to your destination, then adjust your heading accordingly.

Summary of Simple Navigation

Now let's summarize the process of storing your present location and using your GPS receiver to return to it later.

Setup

1. Before you begin, make sure the north reference setting on your GPS receiver is set to TRUE.

2. Set the declination adjustment of your compass to your local declination. Check a recent topo map or the NOAA website if you don't know the local declination.

At the Trailhead

1. Turn on your GPS receiver and wait for it to acquire a position fix. Confirm it is operating in 3D mode, not 2D mode.

2. Decide on an easy-to-remember waypoint name such as "START" for the trailhead or "CAR" for your car. Call up your receiver's waypoint list and delete any existing waypoint with the same name.

3. To store your present location, select the MARK function. Do this by pressing the MARK button (if your receiver has one), selecting MARK from the appropriate menu page, or using the MARK shortcut (if your receiver has one).

4. When the MARK WAYPOINT page is displayed, change the waypoint name from the default number to the name you have chosen.

5. Select the command to store the waypoint. On Garmin receivers, it is usually the choice labeled OK. On Magellan receivers, it is labeled SAVE.

6. Call up the waypoint database and confirm that your waypoint has been stored.

When Ready to Return

1. Turn on your receiver and wait for it to acquire a position fix.

2. Select the GOTO function. Some receivers have a dedicated GOTO button. Others require that you use the FIND function to choose a specific waypoint from the database, then select the choice labeled GOTO.

3. On the receiver's compass page, note the distance and bearing to your destination.

Navigating Back to Your Starting Point

1. Set your compass so that the GPS bearing to your destination is aligned with the direction-of-travel indicator.

2. Hold the compass in front of you at waist level with the direction-of-travel arrow pointing directly away from you. Rotate your body until the magnetic compass needle aligns inside the north reference indicator. The direction-of-travel indicator now points toward your destination.

3. Pick a reference point within the line of your bearing and follow the guidelines for commonsense navigation on page 54. When you arrive at the reference point, take another bearing with your GPS and repeat the process until you reach your destination.

For some people, this may be all you need to know about GPS navigation. If you only want to find your way back to your starting point or store the locations of places you've already been to, you don't need to worry about things like latitude and longitude or how to enter coordinates from a map. Knowing how to mark and go to waypoints may be all you need. But if not, the next chapters show you how to use a GPS receiver in more ambitious journeys.

Part II
Navigation for the Outdoor Explorer

Key Concepts

- ▶ Basics of latitude and longitude
- ▶ Position formats and datums
- ▶ UTM grid
- ▶ How to enter waypoint coordinates into a GPS receiver
- ▶ Understanding topo maps and software maps
- ▶ Planning routes with GPS and maps

Knowing Your Position

If you want to use GPS to do more than simply return to places you've already been, you need to know how to enter waypoints into your receiver without going to them. To do this, you first need to understand latitude and longitude. Hikers and backpackers will also want to know the Universal Transverse Mercator (UTM) system, described later in this chapter. Chapter 5 covers how to enter waypoint coordinates into your receiver.

Latitude and Longitude

You might already be familiar with the concept of latitude and longitude as a way to describe your position anywhere on earth. Originally developed by sailors to guide them across oceans, it divides the earth into lines of latitude, which indicate how far north or south of the equator you are, and lines of longitude, which indicate how far east or west of the prime meridian you are.

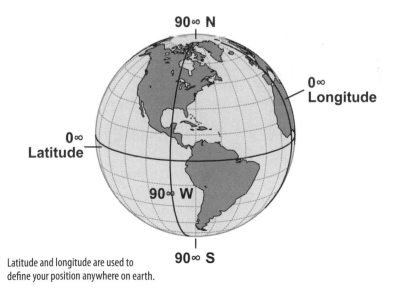

Latitude and longitude are used to define your position anywhere on earth.

The equator is defined as 0° latitude, the North Pole as 90° north latitude, and the South Pole as 90° south latitude. A complete description of latitude must always include the hemisphere—either north or south. If you only report latitude as 34° without indicating the hemisphere, you could equally be describing the latitude of Los Angeles, California, or Santiago, Chile. All locations in the U.S. are north latitude.

Latitude lines are always parallel to the equator, so they are called *parallels*. They become smaller in diameter as you move north or south from the equator, but the distance between them remains the same regardless of where you are on the globe.

Longitude lines are called *meridians*. They are circles perpendicular to latitude that run from pole to pole. Unlike latitude, all lines of longitude are the same diameter. They are called great circles because they are the largest diameter circles you can draw around a sphere. Longitude lines all come together at the poles, so the distance between them gets smaller as you move away from the equator.

Longitude doesn't have a convenient natural reference point equivalent to the equator for latitude. So the location of 0° of longitude, called the prime meridian, is entirely arbitrary. Since the English were the dominant navigators of the 18th century, they chose to define it as the line that runs through the Royal Observatory at Greenwich, England. With only minor changes and the objections of the French notwithstanding, this definition was officially adopted at the 1884 International Meridian Conference in Washington, D.C. The recalcitrant French, though, pouted for another 27 years before they grudgingly abandoned Paris as the site of their prime meridian.

Longitude is a number from 0° to 180° east or west of the prime meridian. Any individual longitude line is only half a circle that runs down one hemisphere from the North Pole to the South Pole. The other half of the same circle, running up from the South Pole to the North Pole, is different in number and opposite in hemisphere. As with latitude, don't forget to specify the hemisphere, either east or west. In the U.S., all lines of longitude are west longitude.

Position Formats

Let's look at how you could describe a position using latitude and longitude. For our example, we'll use the location of the famous Delicate Arch at Arches National Park in Utah. Delicate Arch is north of the equator at latitude 38 degrees, 44 minutes, 37 seconds. It is west of the prime meridian, at longitude 109 degrees, 29 minutes, 58 seconds. When describing a position, latitude comes first. You can write the hemisphere either before or after the number. Most people put it in front. Here's how it would look:

N38° 44′ 37″
W109° 29′ 58″

This commonly used position format is known as hemisphere-degrees-minutes-seconds. It is similar to how we describe time. Each degree is divided into 60 minutes, and each minute is further subdivided into 60 seconds. A degree of latitude represents a distance of about 69 miles anywhere on earth, so 1 second of latitude represents a distance of 101 feet.

For longitude, it's more complicated. The distance between lines of longitude decreases as you move north or south of the equator. In the U.S., for example, 1 second of longitude ranges from about 87 feet in Jacksonville, Florida, to about 64 feet in Seattle, Washington. Many GPS receivers can display latitude and longitude to a tenth of a second resolution. That's a resolution of about 10 feet in latitude and, for U.S. locations, between 6 and 9 feet in longitude.

Although the degrees-minutes-seconds format is commonly used, there are other formats, and you need to know how to tell the difference. If your friend gives you the location of a geocache in one format, for example, and you think it's in another, you'll never find it. One of the most common errors made by experts and novices alike is to incorrectly identify the latitude-longitude format of a position they have been given.

A second position format, known as hemisphere-degrees-decimal minutes, is becoming increasingly popular. It is the preferred format for reporting geocaches. In this format, the number of seconds is converted to fractional numbers of minutes. (You do this by dividing the number of seconds by 60 and adding the result to the number of minutes.) The

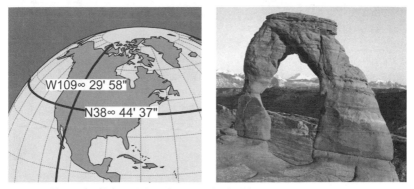

Latitude and longitude of Delicate Arch, Arches National Park, Utah

position of Delicate Arch in the hemisphere-degrees-decimal minutes format looks like this:

N38° 44.617´
W109° 29.967´

A third, less common position format is known as hemisphere-decimal degrees. It goes one step further and converts the number of minutes into fractions of a degree. Again, divide decimal minutes by 60 and add the result to the number of degrees. The position of Delicate Arch looks like this in the hemisphere-decimal degrees format:

N38.74361°
W109.49945°

If you've been given GPS coordinates from someone else or have gotten them from a book or the Internet, make sure you understand their position format. It's easy to get confused because many times the symbols for degrees, minutes, and seconds aren't written down. In that case, you have to figure it out by looking. If it is a set of three numbers separated by spaces, you know it is degrees-minutes-seconds, even if the last number has a decimal point with a number after it—that is just fractions of a second. If it's a set of two numbers, the second having a decimal point and subsequent digits, you know it is the degrees-decimal minutes format. And if it's just one number with a decimal point and subsequent digits, you know it's the decimal-degrees format. To confuse things further, some computer printouts show a single long number of six or seven digits without any spaces or decimal points, a short-form method for the degrees-minutes-seconds format. Computers also often represent north and east by "+" signs and south and west by "–" signs.

Your receiver can select from among the different latitude-longitude formats, along with a number of other position formats. Here's how the different latitude-longitude choices are displayed:

Format	Garmin	Magellan	Lowrance
Deg-min-sec	hddd°mm'ss.s"	DEG/MIN/SEC	Deg/Min/Sec
Deg-dec minutes	hddd°mm.mmm'	DEG/MIN/MMM	Degrees/Minutes
Decimal degrees	hddd.ddddd°	DEG/DDDDD	Degrees

Once you select a position format, your receiver automatically converts the coordinates of any existing waypoints to the new format. But if you're entering new waypoints, you need to make sure your receiver is set to the correct position format before you begin to enter numbers—another very common mistake that can result in large errors. Remember: Your receiver always assumes that any new waypoint is being entered in the currently defined position format. Once the data is entered, your receiver always maintains a waypoint at the same physical location on earth, regardless of how you later change formats. The only way to correct a mistake is to first set your receiver to the correct position format and then reenter the data.

To drive the point home, let's go back to the example of Delicate Arch. Recall that in the degrees-minutes-seconds format, the latitude of Delicate Arch is:

N38° 44′ 37.0″

Select a Position Format

hddd.ddddd°

hddd°mm.mmm'

hddd°mm'ss.s"

Austrian Grid

You can configure your GPS receiver to display coordinates in a number of formats. This example is the display on the Garmin Dakota.

Now suppose you didn't realize your receiver was set to degrees-decimal minutes format, and you used the above data to incorrectly enter its latitude as:

N38° 44.370′

This has the same digits but it's the wrong format. (The correct value for the degrees-decimal minutes format would be N38° 44.617′.) You've just introduced an error of about 1500 feet! You can't fix the problem just by switching your receiver to the degrees-minutes-seconds format after you have entered the data. You have to first set the correct position format, then go back and edit the coordinates to the correct numbers.

The UTM Grid

All maps suffer from a common problem: They must represent the three-dimensional surface of the earth on a two-dimensional sheet of paper or computer screen. No matter how you handle it, the translation process introduces some distortion. We've all seen maps that try to portray the entire world as a single rectangular sheet, and others that cut it into oddly shaped pieces like the peels of an orange. Distortions are usually most noticeable on lines of longitude. On a three-dimensional globe, all longitude lines are straight, but when they are projected onto the flat surface of a map, some will be straight, others bent.

As we have also seen, the distance between lines of longitude decreases as you move away from the equator. At the equator, a degree of longitude spans about 69 miles, while at the Arctic Circle, it is only about 26 miles. Latitude doesn't suffer this problem. A degree of latitude spans 69 miles (ignoring very minor variations due to the earth's slightly elliptical shape) everywhere on the globe.

This variation makes it difficult to measure latitude and longitude coordinates on a map. Special latitude-longitude rulers have been developed, but as explained in Chapter 7, they are cumbersome to use, especially in the field. The Universal Transverse Mercator, or UTM, grid was developed as a way to make it easier to determine the coordinates of a location on a paper map. As you might imagine, it has its roots in the military, where a similar grid is known as the Military Grid Reference System, or MGRS. It is designed for use with large-scale maps such as the USGS 7.5-minute series.

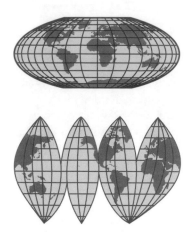

Mapmakers have used many different approaches to project the three-dimensional surface of the earth onto a two-dimensional map. Each one introduces some level of distortion.

The UTM grid divides the entire world from 80° south latitude to 84° north latitude into 60 zones, each covering 6° of longitude. The zones are numbered consecutively, with Zone 1 covering the range from 180° to 174° west longitude. Subsequent zones increase in number every 6° as you move eastward. The continental U.S. is covered by Zones 10

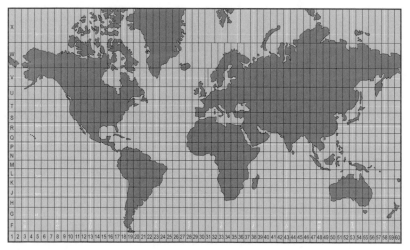

World UTM Zones

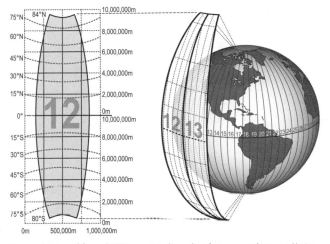

The coordinate grid for each UTM zone is independent from every other zone. Notice how the rectangular UTM grid for Zone 12 extends beyond the zone borders. Only the portion of the grid that lies within the zone represents valid UTM coordinates.

through 19. A rectangular metric grid overlays each zone. However, since the grid for each zone is completely independent of those in other zones, UTM is somewhat complicated to use for travels that stretch across multiple zones.

The grid for each zone is 1,000,000 meters wide, centered on the central meridian of the zone. The entire UTM grid is divided at the equator into two halves. The northern half has its origin at the equator and stretches north to 10,000,000 meters at the North Pole. The southern half is designed so that the equator is at 10,000,000 meters, with numbers decreasing to zero at the South Pole. Neither pole, however, is included inside the UTM system. Instead, a separate grid known as Universal Polar Stereographic, or UPS, covers the polar regions above 84° north and below 80° south. (UPS is outside the scope of this book. If you want to learn more about it, you might try wading through the "Defense Mapping Agency Technical Manual on UTM and UPS" at http://earth-info.nga.mil/GandG/publications/tm8358.2/TM8358_2.pdf.)

The UTM system is designed so that you read horizontal distances eastward and vertical distances northward from reference lines. Not surprisingly, these are called eastings and northings. To measure the coordinates of a location, you first read its distance in meters east of a vertical reference line, then north of a horizontal reference line—a process often expressed as "Read right, then up."

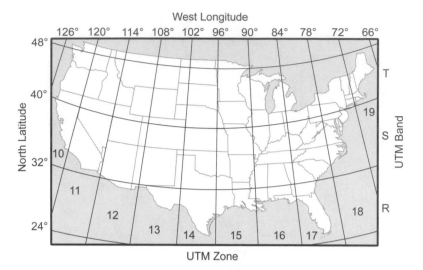

West Longitude

The UTM zone for the continental U.S. spans Zones 10 through 19 and Bands R through U. Each zone spans 6 degrees of longitude and each band spans 8 degrees of latitude.

Each zone is only 6 degrees wide, which means that at the equator, its width is only about 414 miles, or 666,000 meters. Since lines of longitude converge as you move toward the poles, it gets even smaller as you move north or south from the equator, meaning that the rectangular UTM grid extends outside the true zone boundaries on all sides as shown in the figure on page 65. The central grid line of the zone runs straight along the longitude of its central meridian, 3 degrees away from either border. This line is arbitrarily assigned a value of 500,000 meters so that no matter where in the zone you are, you always read a positive easting number. And since the easting boundaries lie outside the confines of the zone, there is no point in the zone with an easting of zero or 1,000,000.

For coordinates in the northern hemisphere, the northing origin is defined as the equator. But if you used this approach for the southern hemisphere, all northing measurements would be negative numbers, which is why the equator is assigned the value of 10,000,000 meters. To keep you from being confused about whether a particular set of coordinates refers to the northern hemisphere or southern hemisphere, each zone is divided vertically into 20 bands of latitude, each 8 degrees high. The bands are assigned letters from "C" at the extreme south to "X" at the extreme north (excluding the letters I and O, which could be confused for 1 and 0), as shown in the figure on page 64. The equator lies at the boundary between Zones M and N. Band X is actually 12 degrees high, an afterthought that came about when the designers realized that 8 degrees wasn't enough to cover the northernmost regions of Greenland. The full UTM coordinates for a point therefore must include the UTM zone number, the vertical band letter within the zone, and a single long number that is the combination of the easting and northing numbers, like this example:

11 S 6456673862920

The "11" means Zone 11, and the "S" means vertical band S within the zone. The single long number is the combination of the easting and the northing. When there are an odd number of digits, the easting number always has one less digit than the northing. So in this example, the easting is 645667 meters and the northing is 3862920 meters. UTM coordinates with fewer digits are less exact. With 13 digits as in the above example, the resolution is 1 meter. With seven digits, the resolution is only 1 kilometer, as in this example:

11 S 6453862

Here, the easting is 645 kilometers and the northing is 3862 kilometers. Note that UTM coordinates are always truncated, not rounded, when they are shortened; the UTM coordinates refer to the lower left corner of a square whose sides are the length of the resolution of the coordinates, not the center of the square. At a given coordinate resolution, every location within this square has the same coordinate value.

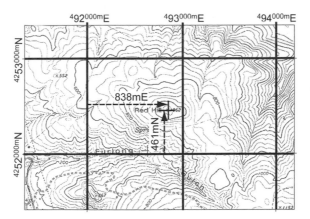

UTM coordinates are designed to "read right, then up." In this example the coordinates of Red Hill are 492838E, 4252461N. The full coordinate description must include the UTM zone number and band letter found on the map margin.

In an attempt to make it easier to read, the easting and northing numbers are often written on separate lines, like this:

11 S 0645667
3862920

That's how your GPS receiver shows the numbers. Notice the leading zero on the easting number so that both easting and northing have the same number of digits.

Sometimes you'll see UTM coordinates written on a single line with easting and northing spelled out:

11 S E645667 N3862920

This is how UTM coordinates are shown on the http://geocaching.com website, for example. Just remember the "E" and "N" are only for clarification. You don't enter them into your GPS receiver. And you'll probably have to enter a leading zero on the easting number.

Topo maps usually abbreviate the UTM number. Since the tic marks occur on 1000-meter increments, there's no need to show the last three zeroes except in the lower left and upper right corners. The digits representing the 1000- and 10,000-meter values are also printed in a larger font. The values in the lower left and upper right corners of the map look like this: $^647^{000}$m E and $^{38}62^{000}$m N. Across the rest of the map, values are abbreviated to look like this: ^{646} and $^{38}63$.

Looking at the illustration on page 65, you can see that the only place where the UTM grid exactly aligns with latitude is at the equator, and the only place it aligns with longitude is on the central meridian of the zone. Everywhere else, there is an angular offset between the two. This difference is called grid north and is usually indicated on a topo map (see the illustration on page 50). Because each zone is 6 degrees wide, the maximum deviation that can occur between grid north and true north is 3 degrees.

USGS topo maps include UTM information either in the form of tic marks on the map neatlines or as a full grid overlay. The USGS map of Half Dome on page 83 includes the full grid. Notice how the gridlines are tilted toward the west, indicating this region lies west of the zone's central meridian.

You may wonder why the UTM system incorporates so many latitude bands when it might seem sufficient to simply use two bands to indicate either "north" or "south" of the equator. In fact this approach would work everywhere except for a few zones in the Nordic regions of Europe. Several latitude bands there have been widened so that Norway and the Svalbard Islands can be accommodated without having to switch zones at inconvenient spots. Some software programs like

National Geographic's TOPO! simplify entry of waypoints by asking only for the hemisphere, either "north" or "south," but you should never use "N" for north or "S" for south when recording a UTM waypoint, because these could be confused with the letter N and S latitude bands, both of which are in the northern hemisphere.

People who have done a lot of hiking with paper maps swear by the UTM system because it is much easier to measure UTM coordinates from a paper map than to measure latitude and longitude. This is certainly true, but UTM has its own limitations. Foremost, it really works best for short journeys that remain inside a single UTM zone—a problem when you plan a trek across more than one zone. Unfortunately for hikers in California's Sierra Nevada, the transition between Zones 10 and 11 cuts right down the middle of the range in the Lake Tahoe area.

Another problem is that UTM isn't at all intuitive. If you come across UTM coordinates for an unfamiliar place, you won't have any idea where it is unless you have committed the system to memory. Take a coordinate beginning with 13T, for example. Is it in Nebraska or Arkansas? At least with latitude and longitude, you have some idea what part of the country you're talking about.

With the coming of electronic maps, the advantages of the UTM system are less pronounced. On your computer screen, it's just as easy to read latitude and longitude as it is to read UTM. And almost without exception, online and printed GPS waypoint coordinates are published as latitudes and longitudes. If you are in the military or belong to a search-and-rescue team, you'll need to know UTM. If you're a serious backpacker, you'll also want to learn it so you can more easily read coordinates from paper topo maps in the field. For the rest of us, it's probably not necessary.

Map Datum

So far, this discussion has covered navigation coordinates as if position format is your only worry. But there's another factor as well: the datum used as the horizontal reference. What's a datum? Well, think back to when you learned geography in school. You might vaguely remember your teacher saying the world is not exactly round; it's really an oval with a bulge in the middle caused by the earth's rotation. The distance from the North Pole to the center of the earth is about 6.5 miles less than it would be if the earth were a perfect sphere. While that distance may not seem like much, it presents a problem for latitude and longitude because they are designed for use on a true sphere. If you didn't correct for this, then 90° north latitude would not be exactly at the North Pole, but rather at a spot in the sky 6.5 miles overhead.

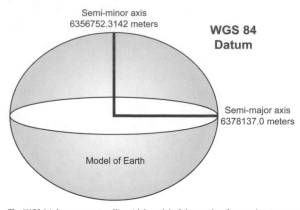

The WGS 84 datum uses an ellipsoidal model of the earth referenced to its center. The older NAD 27 uses a different reference, so the same latitude and longitude coordinates represent a different physical location.

A datum is a model of the earth that allows you to fit latitude and longitude onto its flattened surface. Many different datums have been used over the years by different countries. The two most important for the U.S. are the North American Datum of 1927, known as NAD 27, and the World Geodetic Survey of 1984, known as WGS 84. These datums represent the earth as an ellipsoid, a fancy name for an oval. The Global Positioning System was designed around the WGS 84 datum, but many older topographic maps use NAD 27. Always check your map to see which one it uses. The two datums use slightly different models of the earth, so coordinates expressed with reference to the WGS 84 datum can be as much as 600 feet away from the same coordinates referenced to NAD 27.

Datums are also important for UTM users, since UTM is referenced to latitude and longitude (recall that the centerline of each UTM zone aligns exactly with a degree line of longitude). Since most USGS topo maps are referenced to NAD 27, this datum is most commonly associated with UTM coordinates. But some newer maps are referenced to WGS 84, so always verify the datum of your coordinates.

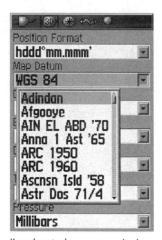

Know how to change your receiver's active map datum. On this Garmin GPSMAP 60CSx, you select the datum from the SETUP menu under the UNITS submenu.

You should always verify the datum setting in your receiver. You'll usually find it in one of the menus under the SETUP page. There will be only one choice for WGS 84 (it may also list NAD 83, which is a virtually identical datum), but there may be many choices under NAD 27. If so, choose the one labeled NAD 27 CONUS for "continental U.S." The other NAD 27 choices are regional variations. There will also be many other choices, with strange names like "Viti Levu 1916" and "Timbalai 1948." Unless you are an archaeologist using antiquated maps or you travel extensively outside the U.S., you'll probably never use most of them.

Entering
and Navigating
to Stored Waypoints

Once you understand latitude and longitude and UTM, you're ready to step up to the next level of navigation skills: programming the coordinates of a waypoint into your GPS receiver without out first going to that location. This chapter assumes you have obtained the coordinates from a friend, the Internet, or another published source. If so, all you need to know is how to enter them into your receiver. Later, in Chapter 7, you will learn the more advanced technique of plotting your own course by reading coordinates from a map.

Geocaching is a typical example of the kind of navigation covered here. Geocaching websites provide the locations of thousands of caches hidden throughout the world by people like you and me. Fans of the sport log onto one of these sites and use its search tool to get a list of all the caches in their immediate area. They then record the waypoint coordinates for any sites of interest and enter them into their receiver. Much of the fun comes in using the receiver to guide them to the cache. The rest comes from discovering the prizes contained within. Geocaching is covered in more detail in Chapter 11. In this chapter, you'll see how to enter coordinates into your receiver and how to navigate more complex routes.

Obtaining Waypoint Coordinates

The first step is to obtain the coordinates of the places you want to go. For geocachers, this step is easy. Numerous websites list the exact WGS 84 latitudes and longitudes of thousands of hidden caches; geocachers can simply copy down and enter these coordinates into their receivers. If you're not a geocacher, you'll have to look elsewhere. Books are one possible source. Hiking guides often publish coordinates for trailside campsites or other points of interest. The Internet can also be useful well beyond geocaching. Numerous sites give you coordinates of just about any place you can think of throughout the world. Internet websites come and go with great regularity, but here are two sites that will probably be around awhile.

The first page, http://gpsinformation.net/main/waypts-2.htm, provides links to many waypoint lists. The other is the Geographic Names Information System, or GNIS, operated by the U.S. Geological Survey. It lists the latitudes and longitudes for more than 2 million place names in the U.S. and its territories. The GNIS home page is http://geonames.usgs.gov/index.html. From there, click on "Search Domestic Names" and enter the name of the feature you are looking for. Once you have found it (many similarly named features may be listed), you can click on various mapping services on the right side of the page to pull up a topo map, highway map, or aerial photo of the spot.

The map datum for the GNIS site has recently been changed from NAD 27 to NAD 83, a datum virtually identical to WGS 84. Be aware the coordinates are read from USGS 7.5-minute topo maps, so they may only be accurate to 5 seconds—about 500 feet in latitude, and a little less in longitude.

Most waypoint coordinates you are likely to come across are reported as latitudes and longitudes, although sometimes you'll see them

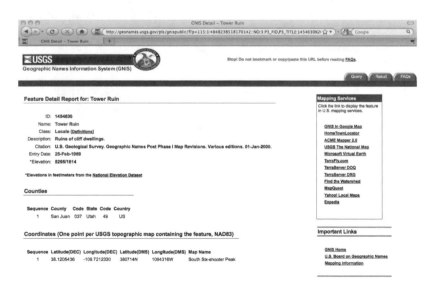

The U.S. Geological Survey Geographic Names Information System (GNIS) website provides the ability to find latitude and longitude coordinates of more than 2 million physical and cultural features within the U.S. and its territories. The NAD 83 map datum used on this site is essentially identical to WGS 84. Note the coordinates are displayed in the decimal-degrees format.

reported in UTM (UTM is most likely to show up in hiking and back-packing magazines or guidebooks). Remember that your GPS receiver knows how to convert from UTM to latitude-longitude and back; even if you don't understand the UTM system, you can still use it. Just set your receiver's position format to UTM and enter the number/letter combinations exactly as given. Once you've done that, switch your receiver back to latitude-longitude if you like.

Organizing Waypoint Coordinates

Once you have the coordinates for all the waypoints you want to program into your receiver, you need to do some basic housekeeping chores:

1. Determine the map datum for the coordinates. Usually it's either WGS 84 or NAD 27. If you have multiple waypoints with a mix of datums, group all the WGS 84 waypoints together in one set and all the NAD 27 waypoints together in a second set. If you have waypoints referenced to the NAD 83 datum, just treat them as if they were WGS 84.

2. Verify the position format for the coordinates. Usually it's either hemisphere-degrees-decimal minutes or hemisphere-degrees-minutes-seconds. Again, if you have a mix of formats, group all of one format together in one set, all the others into another set. If you have a mix of datums and position formats, you will typically have no more than four separate sets of waypoints. If your coordinates also include some in UTM and some in decimal degrees, it could be as many as eight.

3. Decide on the name you want to assign to each waypoint and write it next to its waypoint coordinates. Check to see if a waypoint of the same name already exists in the receiver's database. If so, edit the coordinates of the existing waypoint rather than creating a new waypoint from scratch.

Programming Waypoint Coordinates

Now you're ready to enter the data into your GPS receiver. If you have multiple waypoints, make sure the batteries in your receiver are fresh because the process can take awhile. It's not necessary to be locked onto satellites when entering waypoints, so you can do this job indoors. In fact, even if you are outside, you will save considerable battery power by setting your receiver to the GPS OFF mode (sometimes called DEMO), a choice usually found on the SETUP page.

Before entering the data, go to your receiver's SETUP page and check the setting for both the map datum and the position format. If either of them isn't the same format as your data, change your receiver's setting—otherwise you'll have to start over.

You'd think that manufacturers would make it easy to enter waypoints by providing a choice labeled something like CREATE WAYPOINT. But few receivers provide such a key. Instead, you have to use the same MARK key you use to store your current position, and then remember to edit

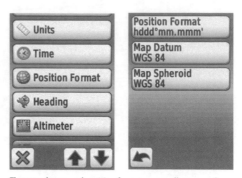

The map datum and position format are usually accessed from the SETUP page. The position format on this Garmin Dakota is set to DEGREES-DECIMAL MINUTES and its map datum to WGS 84. This receiver uses the WGS 84 ellipsoid as its elevation reference (see page 85 for more about elevation measurements.)

the location before you save it. Since the actual process varies by receiver, study your instruction manual for specific details. The general sequence looks like this:

1. Call up the MARK page.

2. Highlight the waypoint's number and change it to the chosen name.

3. Highlight the coordinates and edit them to the correct position.

The method for creating waypoints on this Garmin GPSMAP 60CSx is typical of many receivers. Start by pushing the MARK button as if you were storing your current location. Then, before saving the waypoint, change the waypoint name and latitude-longitude coordinates to the desired values.

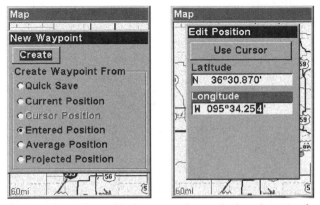

The Lowrance IFinder is one of the few receivers that provides the explicit option of creating a waypoint from scratch rather than starting from your present position.

4. If your receiver allows you to select from a set of symbols, you may want to change the symbol to another choice—a tent symbol for a campsite or a car symbol for the location of your parked car, for example. The advantage is that you can later go back and delete all similar waypoints without affecting other types of waypoints.

5. Some receivers allow you to enter an elevation for the waypoint. This is not a necessary input, so unless you are sure you know it, leave it blank.

6. Store the waypoint by selecting SAVE (Magellan and DeLorme receivers), ENTER (Lowrance receivers), or OK (Garmin receivers).

7. Repeat the process for each additional waypoint.

If all your waypoints use the same datum and position formats, you can enter them one after another. If not, you first need to enter those that match the receiver's current formats, then go back to the SETUP page and change the datum or position format as necessary to enter the remaining waypoints.

No matter what type of GPS receiver you own, entering waypoints directly from the front panel is cumbersome enough that you'll soon want to find an easier way. If you own a computer, you can make the job much easier. All you need is the right software package. In addition to the mapping software programs discussed in Chapter 6, you can use EasyGPS, a free program you can download from the TopoGrafix website at www.easygps.com. The free version gives rather limited capability, with restricted datum and coordinate choices. Purchasing the ExpertGPS upgrade gives you many additional features.

Navigating to Stored Waypoints

You navigate to a manually programmed waypoint using the same approach as described in Chapter 3. First select the GOTO function to find the bearing and distance to the waypoint. Then use your compass to determine the physical direction of that bearing. Finally, head in the indicated direction.

The same cautions also apply: Don't blindly head straight across uncertain terrain. Instead, pick a route that gets you in the general direction without undue risk or damage to the environment. Go around obstacles, not over them. Check your receiver occasionally to get an updated bearing, and adjust your course accordingly. And keep your eyes focused on your surroundings, not your receiver. Pick a target object like a tree or boulder in the distance and use it as an intermediate goal. When you get to it, use your receiver to update the bearing to your destination and continue the process until you arrive. If you're not sure how to follow a bearing, go back and read Chapter 3 in detail.

One added complication is that you often won't have a good idea of your target waypoint's location. If it's a hidden geocache, for instance, you might not even know exactly where to park your car before beginning your search. More than once, I've parked at what I thought was a good starting point, only to find my way blocked by fence lines, cliffs, or rows of houses. It's often a good idea to get a general idea of the waypoint's location before you start out.

If you own a highway or topographic mapping software program that runs on a personal computer, you can enter the waypoint coordinates from the keyboard and view its location on the map display. Zoom in to get a reasonable idea of how to get to the waypoint. Chapters 6 and 7 cover the subject of software maps in detail.

Another option is to use an online mapping service. One good free source is Google Maps at www.google.com. From the Google home page, click on Maps and enter the latitude and longitude coordinates of the waypoint

If you have a mapping receiver you can use its internal map to get some idea of a destination's location. The built-in basemap probably won't be sufficient; you'll need to download a more detailed map from software sold by the receiver's manufacturer. This Garmin Rino has been loaded with data from the MapSource Topo software. No map is without error. The correct name of the lake shown on this map is Ilsanjo.

in any of the three position formats. Begin the entry with the hemisphere and put spaces between the numbers for degrees, minutes, and seconds. For example, the latitude for Delicate Arch in degrees-minutes-seconds would look like this: n38 44 37. You can choose from street, topographic, or satellite views of the location.

Another good free source is MyTopo (formerly Maptech) at http://mapserver.mytopo.com/homepage/index.cfm. Select the "Advanced Search" option and enter the waypoint coordinates in either degrees-minutes-seconds or decimal degrees. If using decimal degrees, enter a minus sign in front of longitude to represent the western hemisphere. The result will be a digital USGS 7.5-minute map of the general area, but the desired spot won't necessarily be at the center of the page. Move the cursor while watching the latitude-longitude displays until it is over the desired position. You can also change the drop-down menu to use UTM coordinates, if you prefer.

The MyTopo server uses the NAD 27 format, so if your waypoints are referenced to WGS 84, you need to convert them, which is easy enough to do. Simply enter them into your receiver in WGS 84 format, and then change the receiver's map datum to NAD 27 to display them in the latter format. Be sure to set the datum back to WGS 84 when finished.

The free EasyGPS program described here also has the ability to link directly to the TopoZone server. It places a crosshair at the waypoint's location on the online map.

Finally, you have the tried-and-true option of using paper maps. You'll need one with a latitude and longitude scale or UTM grid such as a USGS topo map. It's a little more difficult to get an accurate reading from a paper map, but you can easily get a general idea just by looking. Often, that's enough to get you to a good starting point. For more precise information, see Chapter 7, which covers the subject of route planning with paper maps.

6

Topographic Maps

Before you can do any serious GPS navigation, you need to understand maps. With the right map you can:

▶ See how to drive to the trailhead.

▶ Plot a course across the land, either along trails or by cross-country bushwhacking.

▶ Find the latitude and longitude or UTM coordinates of places you want to visit.

▶ Learn the steepness and variability of the terrain you'll be crossing.

▶ Identify obstacles such as rivers or cliffs along your path.

▶ Find your position in the field by comparing physical features of the land to their representations on the map.

Not every map is equally useful. The highway maps you pick up at the local supermarket or auto club are examples of what are called *planimetric* maps. They show towns and highways, and perhaps an occasional railroad or river. But they don't show terrain in any detail at all. Sometimes they plot forests in green or deserts in brown, and occasionally they will show the

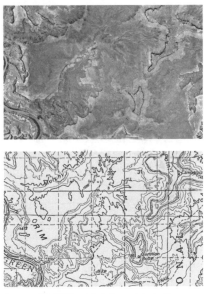

Compare this USGS aerial photograph (actually a composite of two photos) of the region around Junction Butte in Canyonlands National Park, Utah, to the portion of the USGS 1:100,000 topo map for the same location. This same region is pictured in the photo introducing Part II, taken from a point off the lower right edge of the map. (Images courtesy of the U.S. Geological Survey)

location and elevation of a notable mountain peak. But beyond this, you can't tell whether a region is dead flat or steep and mountainous; nor can you read a location's latitude and longitude. Highway maps are great for showing you how to drive to the trailhead, but they are nearly useless once you are out on the trail. What you need in the wilderness is a *topographic* map.

USGS Maps

Topographic, or topo, maps are produced by various government agencies and some private companies. The most comprehensive source is the U.S. Geological Survey (USGS). USGS maps are available at USGS regional field offices as well as at many outdoor shops. You can also order them online directly from the USGS website at http://topomaps.usgs.gov.

The USGS produces several map series at various scales. The most comprehensive are the 7.5-minute series, in which each map covers 7.5 minutes of latitude by 7.5 minutes of longitude. These are the most useful maps for outdoor recreation. It takes about 54,000 maps to cover the entire U.S., including Hawaii but excluding Alaska, which uses 15-minute maps. The scale for 7.5-minute maps is 1:24,000, which means that 1 inch on the map represents 24,000 inches, or 2000 feet, in real life. (A few use a scale of 1:25,000.) These are known as large-scale maps because they cover a small area (less than 10-by-10 square miles) in great detail. It might sound counterintuitive to call a map "large scale" when it covers a small area, but that's the way it's done. Think of it as large scale because it takes a large sheet of paper to show the same area as a small-scale map shows on a small sheet.

USGS also produces topo maps at several smaller scales, including 1:100,000, 1:250,000, 1:500,000, and 1:1,000,000. These show larger areas but in less detail than the 7.5-minute series. The USGS used to produce a series of 15-minute maps, but ongoing budget pressures caused these to be discontinued ("abandoned" in USGS parlance, as if they were dropped off at a homeless shelter somewhere). Today, 15-minute maps are produced only for Alaska.

Fifteen-minute maps of the continental U.S. were drawn at a scale of 1:62,500, where 1 inch represented a little less than 1 mile. Not until they mapped Alaska, did the USGS settle on the more practical scale of 1:63,360, which looks like a strange number but results in a map where 1 inch represents exactly 1 mile.

Fifteen-minute maps were a convenient scale for hikers, but less useful for mining and oil exploration, so when cuts had to be made, it was the 15-minute series that was abandoned. Several private companies

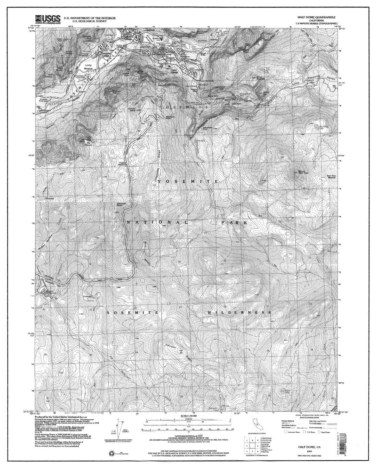

Example of USGS 7.5-minute topographic map

sell updated versions of the old 15-minute series for national parks and other popular hiking areas, although they don't always print them at the standard scale. Remember that USGS maps are often 10 or more years old; don't depend on them in areas that have seen recent development. Learn more about USGS topo maps at http://egsc.usgs.gov/isb/pubs/booklets/usgsmaps/usgsmaps.html.

Topo Map Basics

A topo map not only shows natural and human-made features in more detail than a planimetric map, it also displays the physical shape of the terrain. It does this by way of contour lines representing paths of constant elevation of the land. Knowing the contours of the terrain, you can determine whether your intended route is relatively flat or will climb 2000 feet. You can also determine how the route changes in elevation—a path that repeatedly climbs and descends 100 feet at a time can be more strenuous than one that slowly but steadily climbs the same amount in a single run.

Contour Lines

Most topo maps show contour lines in brown ink. To make them easier to read, every fifth line, called an index contour, is printed in bold and its elevation is labeled. Make sure you know whether the numbers are in feet or meters.

To understand the concept of contour lines, think of an egg slicer—that handy kitchen gadget used to cut eggs, grapes, strawberries, and the occasional finger into neat stacks of slices all the same thickness. Imagine a gigantic egg slicer, its cutting wires spaced 40 feet apart, turned sideways so it can slice horizontally through a mountain. If you looked from the top down after it was sliced, the outline of the mountain at each cut would represent its contour at that elevation.

Depending on the steepness of the terrain, you might want to change the distance between the cutting wires on your giant egg slicer. In relatively flat areas, 40 feet might not give you enough resolution, so it's more useful to set the wires only 10 or 20 feet apart. In very steep areas, you might want an even greater spacing, perhaps 60 or 80 feet.

In the same way, the contour interval chosen by a mapmaker depends on the local topography. Maps covering mountainous areas adopt larger contour intervals than those covering fairly flat regions. The contour interval is always printed somewhere on a map, usually near its scale rule. Pay attention, because it's not always the same even among different maps from the same series. Some USGS maps, for example, report contour intervals in feet, while others are in meters.

By studying the shapes of the contour lines, you can learn information about the land. Lines that are close together represent steep slopes.

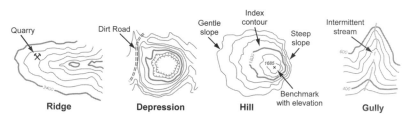

Examples of contour lines and other features found on a topographic map

Widely spaced lines are gentle slopes. Mountain peaks are represented by concentric rings. V-shaped lines pointing uphill indicate a canyon or gully. V- or U-shaped lines pointing downhill indicate a ridge. To help you interpret the various symbols on a topo map, the USGS produces a handy pamphlet entitled "Topographic Map Symbols." You can get a copy at http://egsc.usgs.gov/isb/pubs/booklets/symbols.

Practice reading topo maps by picking up a map of a nearby area. Study the map, then take it out on a trip to see how it relates to the landscape's physical features.

Elevation

Topo maps represent elevation with respect to something called a vertical datum, which is the "zero elevation" reference—usually defined as mean sea level, or MSL. Seems simple enough, right? Unfortunately, it's not. When you are at the beach, you can easily measure sea level, but if you're at a peak in the Rocky Mountains, you don't have that luxury.

There are two ways to define MSL when you don't have an ocean conveniently located nearby. The first is to define it as the elevation at which the force of gravity is the same as at actual sea level—where sea level would be if the land wasn't in the way. Topo maps use this definition. This line of constant gravity, called the geoid, is not a flat surface. It varies irregularly, depending on the shape of the land and the density of the rocks in the immediate vicinity. The change in local gravity caused by the mass of the mountains makes mean sea level higher than it would be if the mountains weren't there.

The other way to define mean sea level is to model it mathematically. Most models represent the earth as an ellipsoid (sometimes called a spheroid). In this case, MSL is the height of the ellipsoid that best matches the true shape of the earth.

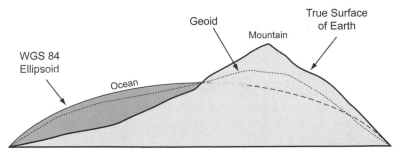

Maps report elevations with reference to mean sea level as defined by the earth's geoid. GPS receivers often measure elevation with respect to the WGS 84 ellipsoid, which only approximates mean sea level.

The standard ellipsoid adopted by GPS is the WGS 84 vertical datum. (Latitude and longitude reference the WGS 84 horizontal datum). Mathematical models are convenient for GPS receivers, but they only approximately represent the true geoid. Depending on your location, the two can differ by more than 300 feet. Across the continental U.S., the geoid ranges from about 10 feet above to 100 feet below the WGS 84 ellipsoid.

The scientific community has only recently spent much time trying to understand the earth's geoid. The most current geoid of the continental U.S. is known as GEOID09. It is based on millions of gravimetric measurements made across the country. Expensive commercial GPS receivers use GEOID09 as their elevation reference, but consumer units often use the less complicated but also less accurate WGS 84 ellipsoid—one reason GPS elevation accuracy is worse than horizontal accuracy. You can learn more about GEOID09 by visiting the NOAA web page at www.ngs.noaa.gov/GEOID/GEOID09.

Understanding Topo Maps

While the "Topographic Map Symbols" pamphlet explains much about the map, it won't tell you everything. Map borders are full of information of varying usefulness. Let's look at the most important information on a USGS 7.5-minute paper map.

Lower right margin. Look here for the name of the map and its date of publication. There's also a simple legend limited to road symbols. Newer printings include an ISBN bar code.

Lower center margin. Here is the map scale, contour interval, and the vertical datum reference. Don't confuse the vertical datum, used only as an elevation reference, with the much more important horizontal datum (see below), which is used as the position reference. Coastal maps also include depth and shoreline information.

Lower left margin. Buried among such details as hydrographic data and grid tick information is the all-important horizontal datum. On most USGS maps, this is the 1927 North American Datum, or NAD 27. Although it doesn't say so, maps of the continental U.S. use what GPS receivers often call NAD 27 CONUS, whose reference point is a physical location on the Meades Ranch in Kansas. Some newer maps also give instructions on how to translate coordinates to the NAD 83 datum, which is virtually identical to WGS 84.

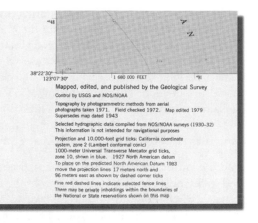

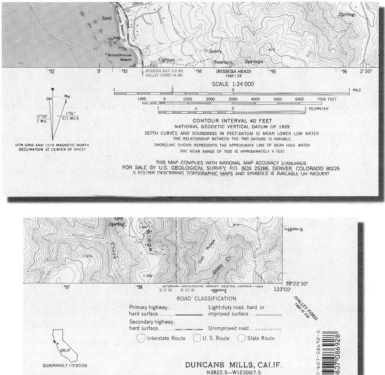

Information on a USGS 7.5-minute topographic map: lower left margin (top), lower center margin (middle), lower right margin (bottom)

Neatlines. The borders of the map, called neatlines, always align with either an even minute or a 30-second line of latitude or longitude. Along the neatlines are numbers relating to various coordinate systems. Latitude and longitude are shown in degrees-minutes-seconds format. The full numbers are printed at the map corners, but only the minutes and seconds are listed in between. Numbers for other coordinate systems are interspersed along the neatlines, making it a little difficult to identify the intermediate latitude and longitude markings. Look for the numbers with the minutes (') or seconds (") marks after them.

You can read the latitude and longitude of any point using the technique described in the next chapter, and then enter the coordinates into your receiver as a GPS waypoint. If you do this very often, though, you may want to learn the UTM system, because UTM coordinates are much easier to read from a paper map. USGS maps all include blue UTM tic marks along the neatlines, and some maps have full UTM grids printed in blue. You can recognize UTM labels because the leading one or two digits are printed in smaller font than the next two digits.

The remaining black tic marks represent the State Plane Coordinate System. Only the marks nearest the lower left and upper right corners are labeled, with a number in feet. Don't worry about these markings. Unless you are a surveyor, you will have little need for them.

Finally, the names of the eight adjacent maps are centered along the vertical and horizontal neatlines and diagonally in each of the four corners of the map.

Software Maps

Paper maps present several problems. First, each map only covers a limited area, so if your journey takes you any distance, you'll have to carry several of them. Second, it's not all that easy to read latitude and longitude coordinates from the map, nor can you easily determine the exact elevation profile of your planned journey. Will it be a steady climb, or filled with hills and dales? After a little practice studying paper maps, you'll get better at interpreting elevation variations, but it will still take you considerable effort for a hike of any distance. You can overcome all these problems by using software maps.

Today, there are many types of software maps. Most are designed to run on Windows PCs, while a few also have Mac versions. Some even run directly from Internet websites. Some, like Garmin's MapSource (www.garmin.com), DeLorme's TopoUSA (http://delorme.com), or Magellan's MapSend (www.magellangps.com), are designed to load maps directly into compatible GPS receivers. These programs, not only

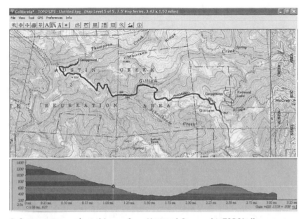

Software maps such as this one from National Geographic TOPO! allow you to plan your route and see its elevation profile. (Map created with TOPO! © 2006 by National Geographic)

let you work from a PC, they also display detailed maps of a region directly on your GPS receiver's screen (albeit on a very small one). Each company uses a proprietary communications protocol that only works with their own receivers.

Other programs are designed to run strictly on a personal computer, but they allow you to transfer waypoints to your GPS receiver by way of a serial or USB cable. These programs work with a wide variety of receivers from many manufacturers, but since they require a computer, they are not practical to carry in the field. They are best used to plan your route ahead of time and then print out a customized topo map for the specific region of your planned travel.

Software maps fall into three categories. The first two, planimetric and topographic, are similar to their paper equivalents. The third category, 3D mapping, is a relatively new development. It adds a qualitative view of topography on top of a planimetric map or aerial photograph.

Planimetric map software is designed for highway navigation. It provides detailed information about roads, freeway exits, and highway mileage. Some can even use voice commands to guide you to exact street addresses. DeLorme's Street Atlas USA is a well-known example. Garmin's City Navigator also fits into this category. As with paper maps, this type of program is great for getting you to the trailhead but of limited use once you are on the trail. Learn more about these maps in Chapter 14.

Topographic map software is much more useful for an actual hike. One type of program starts with scanned versions of USGS topo maps.

These are known as raster graphics maps because of the way the map is digitized. When viewed on the computer screen, the display looks exactly like a digital version of a paper topo map.

The two most widely used raster graphics programs are TOPO! from National Geographic (www.natgeomaps.com/software.html) and Terrain Navigator from MyTopo (http://maptech.mytopo.com/land/terrainnavigator/index.cfm). Both companies offer seamless map coverage of entire states or major recreation areas at resolutions down to the USGS 7.5-minute scale, meaning you don't have to struggle to piece together data from separate paper maps. Both also allow you to measure elevation profiles derived from the USGS digital elevation model (DEM) for each map, making it easy to determine how difficult the hike will be. And both interface with a wide variety of GPS receivers. You can create waypoints and routes in software and automatically upload them to your receiver without having to laboriously enter data by pushing multiple buttons on your receiver. You can also download stored waypoints and tracks from your receiver into the software program so you can see precisely where you have traveled. Chapter 7 explores raster graphics mapping software in more detail.

Another type of program uses what's known as a vector graphics map. Rather than starting from scanned images of paper maps, it stores the shapes of the terrain contours, roads, and rivers as digital lines. This approach greatly reduces the memory required to store a given geography and makes it easier to provide enhanced graphics such as 3D shading, but you may lose other information typically shown on a USGS map. Artificial features such as buildings and trails may have been omitted or even misplaced.

Vector graphics programs offer a similar suite of functions as raster graphics programs. You can create and download waypoints and routes, plot elevation profiles, and transfer data from your GPS receiver into the software program. The efficiency of this type of program is demonstrated by the fact that you can purchase vector-based topo software for the whole U.S. for about the same price as a raster-based program for a single state. DeLorme's TopoUSA is a popular vector graphics mapping program that can also create turn-by-turn driving instructions on the PC. Garmin's Topo and Magellan's Topo USA are two other examples, although they don't offer turn-by-turn highway navigation.

Google Earth (http://earth.google.com) is an example of the relatively new category of 3D maps. It starts with high-resolution satellite photography of the entire earth, then adds additional layers of information, including such elements as road maps, points of interest, and 3D views of terrain and buildings. These views are not accurate enough to

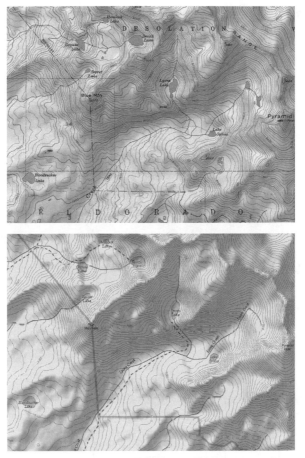

Compare these views of Desolation Wilderness as shown on a raster graphics map (above) and a vector graphics map (below). National Geographic's TOPO! software uses scanned versions of USGS paper maps. DeLorme's TopoUSA uses a digital representation of contour lines and map features. (Maps created with TOPO! © 2006 by National Geographic and TopoUSA © 2007 by DeLorme)

replace a true topo map, and they have other limitations. You can't, for example, see trails in forested areas because the satellite photographs can't look through the trees. However, 3D maps can be useful for getting a general idea of the landscape. We will learn how to combine Google Earth with GPS in the next chapter.

If you browse Internet newsgroups, you'll find strong support for two other programs: OziExplorer (www.oziexplorer.com) and Fugawi Global Navigator (www.fugawi.com/web). These are both very flexible programs that allow you to work with scanned maps from any source. Load any digitized raster graphics map into the program, calibrate it by entering the datum and the coordinates of several map locations, and the program does the rest. You can download waypoints and track logs from your GPS receiver to the computer or upload them from the computer to your receiver. Both programs provide a variety of advanced features.

OziExplorer and Fugawi are different from other programs in that they work with virtually any digitized raster graphics map. With the right maps, they can work worldwide; products such as Terrain Navigator, TOPO!, or TopoUSA provide limited geographical coverage. But this strength is also their weakness. Terrain Navigator, TOPO!, and TopoUSA are complete, turnkey systems that include both maps and software interface. Load the program into your computer and you are immediately ready to go. Neither OziExplorer nor Fugawi include maps—you have to obtain them separately. Some are available from the two companies, and there are many online sites where you can obtain maps free or at a minimal cost. If you have access to a scanner, you can even make your own. If you are technically inclined and comfortable with the Internet, you may find OziExplorer or Fugawi to be the perfect choice. If you just want to get up and running quickly, stick to a turnkey product.

Physical Connections and Interface Protocols

The final thing you need to understand about connecting your GPS receiver to a personal computer is the physical connection and interface protocol. Newer receivers (those introduced within the last few years) connect to a personal computer through the USB interface, a fast, efficient way to transfer maps and data. Older receivers used a nine-pin serial connection known as an RS-232 port. This connector historically came standard with PCs, but has long since disappeared from newer computers. Owners of older GPS receivers with new computers will either have to install a third-party serial card or try to use an external USB-to-serial adapter. Before trying the latter approach, check with the manufacturer of your GPS receiver, as not all adapters seem to work. Garmin offers a USB-to-RS-232 cable designed to work with their receivers.

Even after you've made a good physical connection between the receiver and the computer, you still need to make sure the two are speaking the same software language. It's the equivalent of two people having a conversation in which one person is speaking French and the other is speaking English. Unless they both understand both languages, the conversation will be very difficult. If your receiver has a USB interface and your computer software program can communicate through USB, the job is easy. Simply connect your receiver, launch the software program, and you're up and running.

The problem is a bit more complicated if your receiver doesn't have a USB interface or if you're using an older software mapping program that can't communicate through USB. In this case, you have to use the dreaded RS-232 serial connection. The industry standard for RS-232 communication between GPS and computer is known as NMEA 0183. Developed by the National Marine Electronics Association (www.nmea. org), it defines the formats for messages between the two units. The current version of the standard is 4.0, but your receiver and mapping software should support older versions as well, specifically versions 1.5, 2.1, or 2.3. Both Magellan and Garmin support versions of this standard. Garmin also provides additional proprietary capability, not surprisingly called the Garmin interface protocol. It is supported by most third-party software programs, and in most software, it is the preferred interface for use with Garmin receivers.

One last word of caution: Some receivers designed primarily for marine navigation offer the NMEA 0183 interface, but it is designed to work only with nautical equipment such as autopilots. It won't transfer user data such as waypoints or tracks to a computer. The Lowrance iFinder GO is an example of this type of receiver. Most other iFinder models are compatible with a PC through the removable MMC card.

Route Planning and Navigation

To get the most benefit from your GPS receiver, you need to know how to use it to navigate routes that include intermediate destinations. It's the equivalent of going out for an afternoon of errands: You plan to stop at the post office to buy some stamps, then on to the hardware store and the gym before finishing up at the grocery store and returning home. If you've lived in the area for awhile, you can make the trip by memory. But if you're new in town, you'll probably want to check a map and plan your itinerary. You wouldn't want to go to the grocery store first, leaving your ice cream to melt while you get in a workout at the gym.

GPS Routes

A GPS route is a similar concept. You first enter a series of waypoints, then tell your receiver the sequence you want to travel to them. When you activate the ROUTE function, your receiver automatically guides you to the first destination, as if you had used the GOTO function. When you get there, it automatically guides you to the next waypoint, continuing for each waypoint in succession until you arrive at your final destination.

Think of a route as a series of GOTO functions programmed to occur one after the other. There's nothing you can do with a route you can't also do using the GOTO function for one waypoint after another, but the ROUTE function automates the navigation process. You don't need to memorize the names of a dozen or more waypoints and the order in which you want to reach them. You can also use a route over again without having to check your notes or remember waypoint lists. And most receivers allow you to reverse a route so you can easily get back to where you started.

It's important to know what a route is and how to follow it, but it's not absolutely necessary to use the ROUTE function in your receiver.

Some expert navigators never use anything more than the GOTO function, but if you intend to do any serious wilderness navigation, it is critical that you at least understand how to construct and follow a multileg route. And if you know this, you might as well learn how to use the ROUTE function.

Types of Routes

There are two kinds of routes: open loop and closed loop. An open-loop route is one that goes from a starting point to a destination, traveling through intermediate points along the way. To get back to the starting point, you simply follow the route in reverse, a technique known as reversing the route.

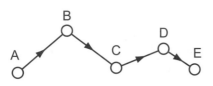
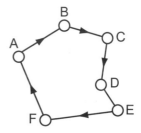

Open-loop route (left) and closed-loop route (right)

A closed-loop route goes from a starting point, through a series of intermediate destinations, and ends up back at the starting point without reversing. The afternoon of errands described at the beginning of the chapter is an example of a closed-loop route—you don't need to return via the hardware store and post office to get home.

Your GPS receiver can handle either type of route interchangeably. In fact, it doesn't even know or care whether the route is open loop or closed loop. It just guides you to a series of waypoints in the order you have told it. The reason you need to know if it is an open-loop route is so you know whether to reverse the route when you reach the end.

Planning a Route with Paper Maps

An example of an open-loop route is the trail to the top of Half Dome in Yosemite National Park. First, let's review the route as shown on the map: Starting at the Happy Isles Trailhead, follow the Mist Trail to the top of Vernal Fall, then continue on to the top of Nevada Fall. There, join the John Muir Trail to its intersection with the Half Dome Trail.

Turn north, taking the Half Dome Trail all the way to the peak. To avoid getting confused by various other trails that enter and depart along the way, you can define a "route" consisting of the trails and the key intersections along the way. Of course, you will eventually want to get back to where you started, but you can do this simply by reversing the route. So your "route" only needs to define the first half of the journey.

To plan the route using USGS 7.5-minute paper maps, you need two maps, *Half Dome, CA* and *Yosemite Falls, CA*. Immediately, you discover the first problem with paper maps: All but a very small part of the trail is on the *Half Dome* map, but you need both maps to see your entire route. The part missing from *Half Dome* is so small, you probably don't want to carry the *Yosemite Falls* map on your hike. But you still need it during the planning process to become familiar with that part of the trail. (You might even want to cut and paste the small portion of the *Yosemite Falls* map onto the *Half Dome* map you carry on the hike.)

First, trace out your route on the map using a pencil or highlighter pen. Then look for the important trail junctions and other points of interest—anything that will help you stay on the right path or lead you to something you want to see. These are the locations you will program into your receiver as waypoints.

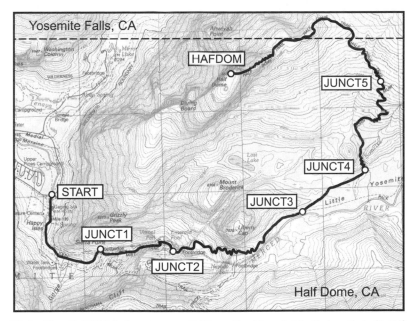

This detail from the USGS 7.5-minute topo maps *Half Dome, CA* and *Yosemite Falls, CA*, shows the trail to Half Dome and possible waypoint locations and names. The dashed line indicates the transition between the two maps. (Map created with TOPO! © 2006 by National Geographic)

The map on page 97 shows seven waypoints, including the starting and ending points. This amounts to a waypoint roughly every mile, which is a reasonable interval. Of course, you should pick waypoints based on how they will help you navigate rather than simply choosing a fixed interval. The example waypoints represent trail junctions where you might make a wrong turn.

For each waypoint, draw a crosshair centered on it to make it easier to accurately read latitude and longitude. Then give the waypoint a name. Make sure it fits within the receiver's naming limitations—some receivers accept waypoint names only up to six characters long; others accept 12 or more characters. Even if they do, shorter names are usually better, especially when using a mapping receiver. You don't want the small map display cluttered with long waypoint names.

Reading Waypoint Coordinates I: Latitude-Longitude

Now comes the challenging part: determining the waypoint coordinates. In this example, you'll see how to measure latitude and longitude, although you could also easily use UTM; the 1997 edition of *Half Dome, CA* has a full UTM grid printed on it. You will learn how to use UTM in the next section.

To read latitude and longitude, you need a special latitude-longitude ruler. Get a nice plastic one at an outdoor specialty shop, or photocopy the one on page 100. Before using it, prepare the map by drawing ruled lines at the 2.5-minute points. Look for the 2.5-minute tic marks along the map neatlines. (There are also crosshairs within the map where these latitude and longitude lines intersect.) Lay down a yardstick and carefully draw lines to connect the corresponding marks on each side of the map. For longitude, extend the lines to the edge of the paper. Do this for both the interior 2.5-minute lines and the longitude neatlines. (You don't need to extend the latitude lines beyond the neatlines.) When finished, your map should look similar to the one in the illustration on the facing page.

Reading latitude is fairly simple. Align the ends of the latitude scale with the 2.5-minute lines on either side of the point you want to measure, making sure the north end of the scale is oriented toward the top of the map. You might need to angle the scale slightly so the two ends align exactly with the 2.5-minute lines. Reading upward from the bottom, the scale shows the incremental latitude in minutes and seconds you must add to the absolute latitude of the lower 2.5-minute line. If your waypoint doesn't align exactly with a line on the ruler, try to estimate its position to the nearest tenth of a second.

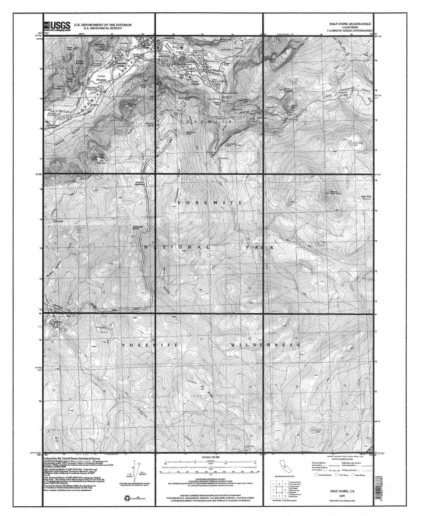

USGS 7.5-minute map *Half Dome, CA*, showing ruled lines necessary to read latitude and longitude

Notice the scale has two sets of numbers, one beginning with 0, and the other beginning with 30. Which set you use depends on the latitude of the lower 2.5-minute line. If it is on an even minute of latitude, use the scale beginning with 0. If it is on a 30-second increment, use the scale beginning with 30. Starting from the latitude at the bottom of your ruler, find the complete latitude of your waypoint by adding the incremental minutes and seconds between this lower latitude line and your waypoint (see the upper figure on the left on page 101). Reading longitude is only slightly more complicated. Remember that the distance

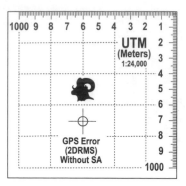

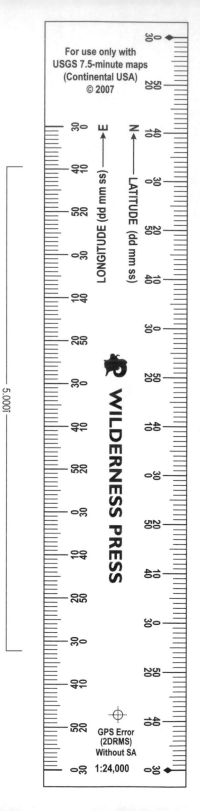

A latitude-longitude ruler (right) and a UTM roamer (above) enable you to read coordinates from a paper map. The ones shown here, which you can photocopy for your own use, are for USGS 7.5-minute maps. Read the text for instructions on their use. You can purchase more sophisticated rulers with markings for many different map scales from a good outdoor specialty shop.

between lines of longitude decreases as you move away from the equator, so it's impossible to construct a fixed-length scale that's right for all maps. But there's still a way—tilt the ruler as shown in the illustration (see upper-right figure on page 101) until both ends align with the 2.5-minute longitude lines, making sure the east end of the scale is on the right. Keeping the scale at this angle, slide it up or down until you can read the longitude of the point of interest. Using the same process as described for latitude, add the seconds and minutes of the longitude coordinate to the longitude of the right edge of the ruler. Repeat this process for the rest of the waypoints you have identified.

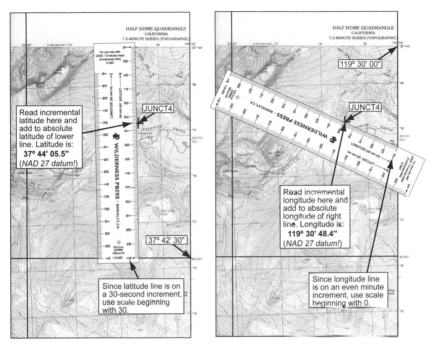

Read latitude (left) by orienting the ruler so the latitude scale aligns with the 2.5-minute lines. (You may have to tilt the ruler slightly.) Orient the scale so the N (north) indicator points up. Add the incremental latitude of the ruler to the absolute latitude of the lower line. In this example, the lower line is on a 30-second increment, so you use the scale beginning with 30.

Read longitude (right) by tilting the ruler so the ends of the longitude scale align with the ruled 2.5-minute longitude lines. Be sure to orient the scale so the E (east) indicator points to the right. Add the incremental longitude of the ruler to the absolute longitude of the line at the right. In this example the right line is on an even minute of longitude, so you use the scale beginning with 0.

Reading Waypoint Coordinates II: UTM

After trying to read latitude-longitude coordinates on a paper map, you will quickly come to appreciate the UTM system. With UTM, you don't need to spread your map out on the ground and tilt a ruler at a crazy angle. You can keep it neatly folded and make your measurements using a small tool called a UTM roamer. Outdoor specialty shops sell plastic roamers calibrated for various map scales, and some compasses even have roamers printed on their baseplates. If you're using USGS 7.5-minute topo maps, you can copy and use the one on the facing page (it works best if you copy it onto transparency material).

Some USGS 7.5-minute maps—like Yosemite's *Half Dome, CA*—come with a full UTM grid preprinted on them, making it easy to read coordinates with your roamer. Others only have UTM northing and easting tic marks printed on the neatlines. If yours doesn't have the full grid, create one by drawing lines to connect the tic marks. The UTM tic marks are easy to recognize because the first digit of the northing and the first two digits of the easting are printed in a smaller font than the next two digits. Lay a yardstick so that it connects the same numbers on either side of the map and use a pencil or fine-tipped pen to draw the connecting lines. (The UTM grid will not be parallel to the neatlines unless the region covered by your map lies near the central meridian of the UTM zone.) When you are finished, your map should look something like the one on page 99.

Now you are ready to read the UTM coordinates of your waypoints. Lay the roamer on the map so that its upper right corner aligns with the waypoint of interest, as shown in the diagram. Make sure the roamer is oriented parallel to the UTM gridlines, not the map neatlines. To read the coordinates, remember the adage, "Read right, then up," meaning read the easting first. Write down the easting value of the map gridline at the left of the waypoint, remembering to append three zeroes to the end. Then read the incremental easting on the roamer where it intersects the gridline. (You have to estimate the last digit by interpolating between the scale markings on the roamer.) Add this number to that of the gridline.

In the diagram, the easting of the gridline is ^{2}78. Append three zeroes to get the number 278000. Since UTM coordinates are expressed in meters, this number represents the number of meters east of the zero reference point of the zone (refer to the illustration on page 65 if you need to review the concepts of the UTM system).

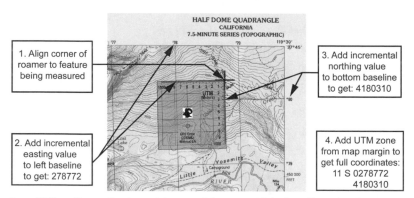

To read UTM coordinates, align the top right corner of the roamer with the desired location on the map. Add the incremental easting and northing values from the roamer to the absolute values from the map, as shown.

Now read the incremental easting of the roamer. In this diagram, it is 772. Add it to the easting of the gridline to get an easting of 278772 for the waypoint. Your GPS receiver will probably want you to add a leading zero to make it 0278772.

Northing values are read similarly, working upward from the reference gridline. In the diagram on page 102, the northing of the gridline is ^{41}80 (note that northings have one more digit than eastings). Append three zeroes to get a northing of 4180000. This is the number of meters the gridline lies north of the equator. Now read the incremental northing on the roamer, 310. Add this to the northing of the gridline to get a northing of 4180310 for the waypoint.

The complete coordinates must include the UTM zone. On a USGS topo map, this number is listed in the lower left corner; the *Half Dome, CA* map is UTM Zone 11. Curiously, the USGS doesn't list the alphabetical latitude band, which happens to be "S" for Yosemite. But don't worry. All you have to know is whether you are north or south of the equator. Then enter the coordinates, and your GPS receiver will automatically determine the correct letter. (Some models don't even let you enter a latitude band, and the ones that do automatically correct it if you get it wrong.) The full UTM coordinates then become:

$$11 \ S \ 0278772$$
$$4180310$$

Since UTM coordinates are expressed in meters, it's easy to use your roamer to measure distances between points on the map. The full length of the scale is 1000 meters, and each minor scale division represents 10 meters. You can interpolate between these minor divisions to read the coordinates of a waypoint to an accuracy of about 5 meters.

Creating the Route

Once you've measured all the waypoints, you're ready to create the route. First, enter the coordinates of each waypoint into your GPS receiver, making sure the map datum and position format are set properly (in this example, they are NAD 27 and either degrees-minutes-seconds or UTM). Now you're ready to create the route. Since the details of how to do this vary among receivers, read your instruction manual for specific directions. In general, the sequence goes something like this:

1. Select the ROUTE page on your receiver.

2. Select NEW or an unused route on the screen.

3. In the first waypoint position, enter the name of the starting waypoint for the route.

4. Continue entering waypoints in subsequent positions in the order you want to go to them.

5. Name the route and save it in the memory.

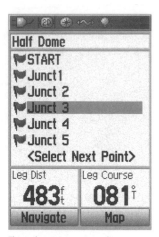

Once a route has been entered and saved, you can use it for navigation. Again, check your instruction manual for details. Typically, you go to the ROUTE page, choose the route you want, and select the key labeled something like NAVIGATE, FOLLOW, or ACTIVATE.

The first waypoint in the route is always your starting point, not your first destination. So when you activate a route, it immediately directs you to the second waypoint, even if you are nowhere near the starting point. You might wonder why you even need to enter the starting point, but remember it becomes very important if you plan to use the route reversal feature to lead you back to the beginning.

This is the route screen on the Garmin GPSMAP 60CSx. As with all receivers, the indicated straight-line distances between waypoints may be significantly shorter than the true hiking distances.

Planning a Route with Software Maps

Route planning with paper maps is tedious, especially when it comes to reading waypoint coordinates. Software maps make the process much easier. You can easily draw your intended route onto the map, read its total length, and generate an elevation profile. You can quickly place waypoints on the route and electronically transfer their coordinates to your GPS receiver. Once you have used software maps, you'll find it difficult to go back to using paper maps.

Let's take a quick look at how you would plan the same route to the top of Half Dome using a software map. This example uses National Geographic's TOPO! State-Series software for California, but the process is similar for other software packages.

After installing the software on your PC, launch the program and zoom in on the area around Half Dome. With TOPO!, the highest zoom level displays USGS 7.5-minute maps. The first difference you'll notice is its seamless coverage. You'll hardly even be aware that the trail stretches across two paper maps. TOPO! also gives you the convenience of selecting coordinates in either latitude and longitude (in any of the

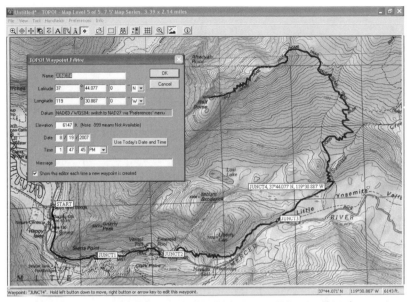

Software maps make it easy to create waypoints and load them into your GPS receiver. This is the waypoint screen from National Geographic's TOPO! software. (Map created with TOPO! © 2006 by National Geographic)

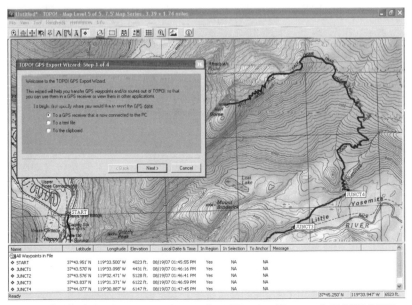

You can easily upload a list of waypoints you've created to a GPS receiver. (Map created with TOPO! © 2006 by National Geographic)

three formats) or UTM, and selecting either the NAD 27 or WGS 84 datum. You access these choices from its PREFERENCES menu.

Next, use the ROUTE tool to draw your intended trail on the display. (Although TOPO! calls this a "route," it is a "track" or "trail" in GPS parlance.) It takes a little practice to draw an accurate trail using TOPO!'s tool. You'll probably need to use the right mouse button to erase mistakes several times along the way. But with care, you'll end up with a reasonable representation of the trail. When finished, click the left mouse button to end the trail. A dialogue box appears that shows the trail's total length, gives you the option of naming it, and allows you to do things like change the line style or build an elevation profile.

Now you're ready to create the GPS route by adding waypoints using the WAYPOINT tool. Click the pointer on each location where you want to add a waypoint and a dialogue box comes up giving you the location and other information. Highlight the name box and type in the desired name. Click OK, and the waypoint will show up on the screen. Do this for each waypoint you want to add. When finished, you'll have a list of waypoints ready to be loaded into your GPS receiver. Connect your receiver to your computer using the appropriate cable, and select the HANDHELDS menu to upload the information—much simpler and more foolproof than using paper maps.

Google Earth and Google Maps

Google Earth and Google Maps are relatively new additions to the array of commercially available mapping software programs. Both are free tools from Google (www.google.com). Neither is a true replacement for a good topo map, but they can be useful supplements. In many ways the two applications are similar. Both show satellite imagery of the entire earth, and both overlay additional information such as roads, points of interest, and street views. A primary difference is that Google Earth runs as a standalone program on either a PC or Mac, while Google Maps runs as a web-based application. Google Earth also includes a more comprehensive set of GPS tools, including the ability to mark waypoints and import GPS tracks, so most people find it the better choice for wilderness exploration.

Before you can use Google Earth, you must install the application onto your computer from http://earth.google.com. Versions are available for both Windows and Mac systems. Once you have completed the installation, you may want to review the tutorials in the HELP menu to learn more about how to use it.

When you launch the program, you first see a photograph of the entire globe, which you can rotate however you like using your mouse.

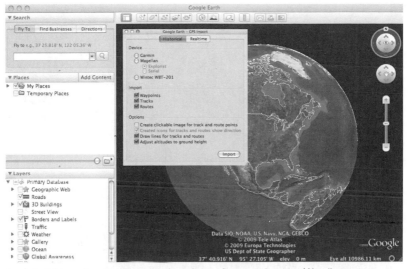

Google Earth lets you import waypoints, tracks, and routes from many Garmin and Magellan receivers.

Use your track wheel to zoom in or out. At the highest level of resolution, you can see individual buildings, cars, and in some cases, even people. Take some time to explore the earth in a way you may never have seen before.

The most recent release of Google Earth allows you to seamlessly import track and waypoint data from your Garmin or Magellan receiver and display it on the screen. (With earlier versions you had to purchase an additional option.) Start by connecting your receiver to the computer's USB port and then select GPS from Google Earth's TOOLS menu. You will see a dialog box from which you can select your receiver and initiate the import. The GPS import function works with many receivers from Garmin and Magellan. Other brands of receivers may work but aren't officially supported. If not, you will need to import the GPS data from your receiver into your computer as a .GPX or .LOC file, then open this file in Google Earth. If you're not sure how to do this, check your receiver manufacturer's website for specific details.

It is also possible to create waypoints (called "placemarks" in Google Earth) and export them to your GPS receiver, but it isn't as easy as going the other way. Google Earth doesn't provide an easy way to export placemarks to any brand of receiver. Here's a quick overview of one way to do it. Start by positioning the placemarks in Google Earth using the PLACEMARK tool (the one that looks like a pushpin). You can zoom in and drag the placemark around on the map, or if you know the desired latitude and longitude coordinates, type them into the dialog box. The

You place waypoints in Google Earth using the Placemark feature. You can either drag the pushpin to the desired location or type its latitude-longitude coordinates in the box. Refer to the text to see how to export these waypoints into a GPS receiver.

dialog box is also where you give the placemark a name. Once you click OK, the placemark shows up under the "My Places" list on the left side of the screen. Continue until you have created all your placemarks.

It takes two steps to get the placemarks into your receiver. First save your "My Places" data by selecting FILE, SAVE, MY PLACES, which saves your data in a Google-specific .KMZ file format. You must now convert this file to a .GPX file format that can be exported to your receiver. Several websites offer low-cost tools to make this conversion and export the resulting data to your receiver. One good source is the ExpertGPS website at www.expertgps.com/kmz-to-gpx.asp. The specific details of how to make the conversion depend on the software tool you use and are beyond the scope of this book. Refer to your tool's website for more information.

Garmin Custom Maps

In November 2009, Garmin released a new feature for their Oregon, Dakota, and Colorado series receivers called Garmin Custom Maps. In conjunction with Google Earth, it allows you to load your compatible receiver with any map you can convert to a JPEG file. You must first create the image, typically either by photographing the map with a digital camera or by using a digital scanner. The JPEG file settings must meet

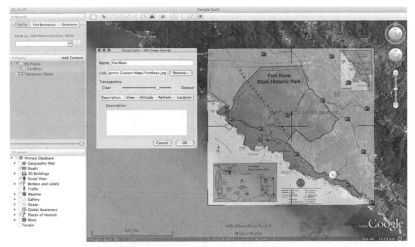

To load a custom map into a compatible receiver using Garmin Custom Maps, you must first create a JPEG file and import it into Google Earth. After aligning the map to features visible in Google Earth, you can export it to your receiver. Here, the official map of California's Fort Ross State Historic Park is ready for export.

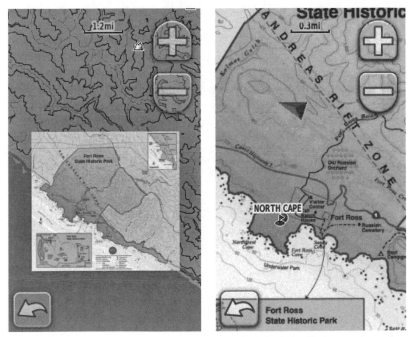

Using Garmin Custom Maps, this Oregon 400t receiver has been loaded with the official state park map of California's Fort Ross State Historic Park. On the left, the map is shown on top of the Oregon's built-in topo map. On the right, the receiver's current location is superimposed on the park map.

certain requirements as defined on the Garmin Custom Maps website at www.garmin.com/garmin/cms/us/onthetrail/custommaps.

Once you have the JPEG map file, import it into Google Earth by selecting IMAGE OVERLAY from the ADD drop-down menu. In the dialog box that appears, give the map a name, set the LINK location to that of your image, and set the DRAW ORDER to 50. Before clicking OK, you must adjust the position and scale of the image so it aligns with the corresponding features in Google Earth—a process called georeferencing. To adjust position, grab and drag the crosshairs at the center of the map. To adjust scale, grab and drag a corner of the map. By default, only the corner you have grabbed will move, which distorts the map. To maintain perspective, hold down the SHIFT key as you drag the corner. To check how well you have aligned the map, adjust the TRANSPARENCY slider in the dialog box so you can look through the image and compare its alignment with Google Earth. When you like how the map is aligned, click OK to save it in Google Earth.

Your map is now ready to be exported to your receiver. Connect your receiver to a USB port and open your computer's file manager dialog box. Select your receiver's drive letter and then open the GARMIN folder. If a subfolder called CUSTOM MAPS doesn't yet exist, create it now. To transfer the map, highlight its name in Google Earth's MY PLACES folder. Right-click its name and then click SAVE PLACE AS. Save your map in the Garmin\Custom Maps folder in your receiver.

Garmin Custom Maps gives you the unique ability to load your receiver with topographic or planimetric maps for any location in the world as long as you have a suitable JPEG map. For example, you can load your receiver with a customized map of a college campus, a shopping mall, or an archaeological dig. Don't expect to achieve pinpoint accuracy, however. You will be limited, not only by how accurately you can align the scanned map in Google Earth, but also by the inherent accuracy of the original map. Many maps weren't drawn accurately enough to be used with GPS receivers, and they often show features far away from their true positions. Even so, Garmin Custom Maps can be a powerful tool as long as you understand and accept its limitations.

Part III
Recovering from Disaster

Key Concepts

▶ Essential items for wilderness travel

▶ Planning ahead to avoid disaster

▶ Basic map-and-compass skills

▶ Wilderness navigation without GPS

▶ Advantages of waiting for rescue versus finding your own way out

▶ Primitive methods for finding your way without a map or compass

Preparing for Disaster

The chapters in this section deal with the inevitable question: "What do I do when I'm out in the wilderness and my GPS receiver fails?" First, let me point out that this is not a book on outdoor survival. If you intend to spend much time in the wilderness, you should know many survival techniques that aren't covered here. Check the references in Appendix II for information on wilderness survival. This section covers alternate navigation techniques—methods you can use to get back to safety if you unexpectedly find yourself without a working GPS receiver.

Essential Items

The best way to deal with disaster is to avoid it in the first place. It doesn't take a lot of preparation to turn what could have been a serious incident into something that's little more than a momentary inconvenience. Many books provide lists of "10 Essentials" that should be carried by every outdoor adventurer. The first list was originally compiled by The Mountaineers back in the 1930s for use by climbers. Updated for today's needs, it is a good list for anyone intending to travel more than an hour or two from civilization. Everything here should fit in an ordinary daypack with room to spare:

1. **Extra clothing.** Even if you plan to go out for only a dayhike, take a few key items of clothing. You primarily need protection against unexpectedly cool and windy weather, and perhaps the occasional rain shower. Check the weather forecast for the next several days and pack the minimum you think you would need if you were stuck overnight. A windproof jacket is essential. Without a windproof shell, an ordinary fleece jacket won't protect you in even moderate winds. The one I carry for emergencies is a lightweight shell that rolls up into a tiny 6-inch stuff sack and weighs less than 9 ounces.

   If rain is even remotely possible, your jacket should be waterproof. Be wary of inexpensive nylon clothing advertised as "water-resistant." Such material isn't designed to keep you dry for extended periods. "Waterproof-breathable" fabric is more expensive but well worth it if you're caught in a downpour.

Long pants and a wide-brimmed hat are also important. Cargo pants with zip-off legs let you easily adapt to changing weather conditions without adding much bulk in a daypack. Other recommended items are an extra pair of socks (in case you get wet crossing a stream), and gloves and a warm hat to help keep you warm if you get delayed overnight. Finally, you should always have an aluminum-coated Mylar "space blanket" stowed for an emergency. It weighs next to nothing and can keep you remarkably warm if necessary.

2. **Extra food and water.** You don't need to pack four-course meals if you're only planning to be out for the morning, but you should always have extra rations to tide you over in an emergency. Energy bars, beef jerky, and freeze-dried backpacker meals (if you have water and a way to heat them) are good alternatives. These rations should be in addition to the food you already planned to bring. Plan so that if nothing goes wrong, you'll still have food left at the end of your journey.

    Carry plenty of water, even in regions where ground water is readily available. These days, you need to purify water from almost all natural sources, so you might want to carry water-purification tablets or a water filter as well. When purchasing a filter, look for one rated to 0.2 micron, which will not only screen out giardia, the most common problem, but other harmful bacteria as well. Note that water filters won't kill viruses unless they also include an iodine treatment—not usually a problem in the U.S. but a definite concern in the third world. Water-purification tablets do kill viruses but flavor the water with a distinctive chemical taste. Tablets don't have an indefinite shelf life and deteriorate quickly after the bottle is opened. Follow the instructions on the bottle to understand proper use.

3. **Sunglasses.** When this list was originally developed in the 1930s, sunglasses were a relative rarity. Now they are routine. Admittedly, they aren't essential in every case, but research has shown that excessive exposure to the sun is associated with eye cataracts and macular degeneration. If you expect to travel over sand, snow, or water, sunglasses are required to prevent temporary or permanent eye damage from reflected sunlight. Make sure they are rated to block 100 percent of both UVA and UVB rays.

4. **Knife or multipurpose tool.** The Swiss Army knife has been the tried-and-true staple for many years. It's still a good choice, but these days many people have come to prefer a multipurpose tool that includes pliers, scissors, screwdrivers, and numerous other implements in addition to the basic knife. Models by Leatherman (www.leatherman.com) and Gerber (www.gerbertools.com) are well-designed, reliable, and priced to match.

5. **Matches and fire starter.** Although you may take a good supply of ordinary matches, make sure you supplement those with specialty waterproof matches. You might also pack a butane pocket lighter. Everyone in your group except small children should carry his or her own supply of matches.

   Even in wooded areas, it might not be that easy to start a fire in an emergency. You don't want to waste all your matches trying to light damp leaves or green pine needles. Solid-fuel tablets or jellied-fuel tubes, available at camping supply stores, can get a roaring fire started with a single match. Even a simple candle can be better than nothing.

6. **Whistle or signaling device.** A simple whistle kept in a pocket or lashed to a backpack works much better than your lungs at calling for help—especially for children, whose voices don't carry very far. The universal signal for help is three short blasts repeated at regular intervals.

7. **First-aid kit.** At minimum, a first-aid kit should include gloves, adhesive bandages, a few larger gauze pads, aspirin or ibuprofen, adhesive tape, antibacterial ointment, a good pair of tweezers, and a first-aid instruction manual. For larger groups or extended trips, the kit should necessarily be larger and more extensive. One generally useful item is a 25-foot length of braided nylon or parachute cord. Check your local outdoor specialty shop for pre-assembled kits, or study their contents to aid in assembling your own.

8. **Flashlight.** As with matches, everyone in a group should carry at least a small flashlight. Those by Mag-Lite (www.maglite.com) are durable and reliable. You may also want to check out some of the newer LED-based flashlights that put out bright illumination with less drain on batteries than incandescent lights. Headlamps also have become popular, as they allow you to keep both hands free for other activities.

9–10. **Map and compass.** As already described, a map and compass are essential any time you venture into the wilderness. Bring a pen or pencil to make notations on the map.

Of course, if you only intend to travel through the local park, a survival kit this extensive is hardly necessary. But the subject of this section is recovering from disaster; if you drop and break your GPS receiver in the local park, it might be a disaster to your pocketbook but hardly something that will keep you from finding your way home. For the kinds of wilderness travel implied in these chapters, every one of these essentials should be in your pack.

GPS Survival Kit

The GPS navigator needs to expand on this list slightly by adding three additional things:

▶ GPS receiver

▶ Sturdy carrying case

▶ Extra batteries

Remember that your GPS receiver does not replace the map and compass, it is in addition to them. You still need the map and compass so you can navigate if your GPS receiver fails. In the next chapter, you'll see how to do this.

It's important to keep your receiver in a carrying case when it is not being used. A GPS receiver is not indestructible, and letting it bang around loosely in your pack or pocket will only hasten its demise. On some receivers, the connections between the LCD display and the internal electronics are particularly susceptible. If you start noticing lines running horizontally or vertically through the display, you'll know the connections are suspect. Sometimes you can temporarily solve the problem by striking the receiver against the palm of your hand (never anything harder), but try that as a last resort.

The carrying case can be one originally designed for a digital camera or one that has been custom-designed for your receiver. The important thing is that it be sufficiently padded to provide reasonable protection.

Extra batteries are an absolute necessity. Stick a few extra AA cells (or whatever your receiver requires) in your pocket or backpack, or in the side pocket of your receiver's case, if it has one. You'll have cheap, lightweight insurance against unexpected power loss. Not having spare batteries in the wilderness should be a criminal offense.

These backup batteries should be alkaline, not nickel-cadmium (NiCad) or nickel-metal hydride (NiMH) rechargeables. Alkalines will not only keep your receiver operating longer (more than twice as many hours as NiCad), they also have a considerably longer shelf life. NiCad and NiMH rechargeables will slowly discharge just sitting on the shelf, and after only a few weeks, they will need to be recharged. Rechargeable batteries are fine for casual use on dayhikes where you have easy access to a charger, but don't rely on them in the wilderness. For cold-weather use, you might even consider lithium batteries. Although they're much more expensive than alkaline, their cold-weather performance is considerably better. See page 207 or check your GPS receiver's instruction manual for more information on battery compatibility.

Other Backup Plans

The more care you put into planning your adventure, the less likely you are to get into serious trouble. In addition to the 10 essentials, here are a few other things you can do to reduce the risk of disaster.

Spare GPS receiver. Aircraft, ships, and spacecraft all have double- or triple-redundant navigation systems. When your life depends on it, you can't allow yourself to be put in jeopardy by a single instrument failure. The serious outdoor navigator would do well to consider the same possibility and invest in a second GPS receiver as a backup.

This recommendation isn't intended to stimulate the economy by helping sell GPS receivers. If your safety doesn't depend on your GPS receiver, if you can find your way home without it, you probably don't need to make the investment. But if you plan a journey into serious wilderness—the wilds of Alaska or the Australian Outback, for example— ask yourself how important it is that you have a working GPS receiver. Spending an extra $100 on a backup receiver may be a minor additional expense compared to the total cost of your trip.

Lightweight models such as the Garmin Geko make it difficult to claim you can't afford the extra weight. Just be sure that if you bring a second receiver, you know how to use it. You don't want to be struggling to learn a new receiver at what is already a time of serious stress. This is one argument in favor of selecting a backup receiver from the same family as your primary receiver. It might not have all the same features, but at least it will have a familiar interface.

There are a couple of other things to remember when bringing a backup receiver. First, make sure it, too, has fresh batteries, and that you have appropriate spares. The Geko, for example, uses AAA batteries. Your primary receiver probably uses AA cells. So you would need to bring some of each.

Second, remember to turn on your backup receiver and mark your position at the beginning of the journey. It's best if you enter all the intermediate waypoints as well. If you get into a situation where you need to depend on a backup receiver to aid your return, you want to make sure it knows where you're going.

If there is more than one person in your party, spread the GPS receivers out among them. That way, if you get separated or someone loses a backpack over a cliff or down a river, you haven't also automatically lost your backup.

Cell phone. Another survival item you might be considering is a cellular telephone. In movies and television ads, such phones always work with crystal clarity. In the wilderness, though, they probably won't. Telephone companies are understandably driven by profit, so they install base stations in locations they know will get used. Wilderness areas aren't at the top of their coverage list.

Unless you know you are going to be within range of a cellular base station, you shouldn't depend on a cell phone to get you out of a fix. You might still bring it along and be pleasantly surprised. In the California desert, I've gotten good reception 50 miles from the nearest habitation and well away from the coverage limits shown on the telephone company's maps. But I always regard such a result as a lucky happenstance and would never trust my safety to achieving a repeat performance.

The new generation of smartphones including the iPhone, Blackberry, and Android includes a built-in GPS capability. Although sufficient for casual use near populated areas, a smartphone is not a substitute for a dedicated GPS receiver. Read the explanation on page 35 for more insight into the limitations of GPS-enabled smartphones.

Share your itinerary. Finally, any time you plan a journey into the wilderness, even if just for a few hours, let someone know your plan and when you intend to return. You never know when an accident might interrupt your travel. If you suddenly find yourself with a serious injury, you might not be able to get back, even if your GPS receiver is still working. If you don't return in a timely manner, at least someone will be aware of your absence and can initiate a search-and-rescue operation if necessary.

Navigating with a Map and Compass

So far, maps and compasses have played only supporting roles in outdoor navigation. As long as you have a working GPS receiver with all necessary waypoints stored properly, you can safely use it as your primary navigation tool. But what do you do if your receiver fails? Perhaps the batteries died and you don't have spares. Or maybe it took a hard blow in a fall, breaking the display. Or even worse, maybe you lost it in a lake or over a precipitous chasm. Now what? How do you get back to safety?

This chapter assumes you've done the sensible thing and brought along a topo map and compass. It also assumes it's not as simple as following a well-marked trail back to your starting point. Perhaps it's been snowing and your tracks are covered. Maybe you've done serious cross-country hiking or spent the day canoeing on a remote, unfamiliar lake. You need to get back using only your map, compass, and navigation skills. This chapter won't teach you everything about map-and-compass navigation, but you'll learn enough to get by in an emergency.

First, stay calm. You've sensibly packed a map and compass, so you're already halfway home. Now relax and remember how to use them. With a map and compass, getting back to safety involves four steps:

1. Determine your present position.

2. Decide on your destination.

3. Identify the best route to get there.

4. Follow the chosen route, making adjustments as necessary along the way.

Determining Your Present Position

Before you can figure out how to get to safety, you first have to know where you are. Don't panic and start heading in a random direction or in what you think might be the right direction without confirming it. Take the time to really identify where you are.

One fundamental skill you should make a habit is to regularly correlate your GPS position with the map. That way, if the receiver fails, you already have a good idea of your location. Unfortunately, too many people fail to do this. How do you find your position when you haven't been keeping careful track? This section describes three ways: triangulation, dead reckoning, and altimeter navigation. But none of these is as good as correlating your position as you travel.

Triangulation

The easiest approach, if the opportunity presents itself, is to triangulate your position from objects you can see in the landscape. It's similar to how your GPS receiver works, but of course you're not using satellites, so you must use identifiable objects in the landscape.

Orienting the map. You first need to orient your map to the surroundings. When you're facing north, you want the top of the map to also face north. That way, it's easy to match a feature in the distance to its corresponding feature on the map.

Do this by using your compass. Set it to an indicated true bearing of 0° and lay the compass pointing north on the map so the side of the compass aligns with a map border (neatline) as shown in the photo. Now rotate your map and compass together until the magnetic needle is boxed inside the north reference indicator. Your map is now aligned to the landscape.

To orient your map to the surroundings, set the bearing indicator to 0° true and align the edge of the compass with the neatline. Rotate map and compass together to box the magnetic needle inside the north reference indicator. Note this compass has been adjusted to compensate for magnetic declination.

This method works only with a compass that's been set to compensate for local declination. Otherwise, you need to make the adjustment by mentally correcting for declination—not something you will want to worry about when you're already stressed from losing your primary navigation tool. This is where you will appreciate a compass with adjustable declination. Now would be a good time to brush up on the principles of declination correction described on pages 50 and 51.

Triangulating your position. Now that you've got the map properly oriented, you're ready to triangulate your position. Here's how:

1. Identify at least two objects (preferably three) in your field of view that are also on the map. These can be prominent mountain peaks, radio towers, waterfalls, or just about anything else you can reliably identify in both your surroundings and on the map. Ideally, the objects should be at close to right angles from each other, though this is not always possible. Avoid objects that are in line or 180° apart.

   If you happen to be on a known river, trail, ridge line, gully, or similar geographic feature, you only need to identify one additional object (preferably two). You can use these features, known as *hand-rails*, to help identify your position.

   If you can't spot suitable objects from your current position, do a little reconnaissance. Climb to the top of a nearby hill (if you can do it safely) or move to an area with a better view—a meadow or forest clearing, for example. Be cautious when moving, and don't lose visual contact with others in your party.

2. Use your compass to read the bearing to each object. (If you need a refresher on taking a bearing, refer to page 53.) You will plot these bearings on the map, so they need to be referenced to true north. Again, investing in a compass with adjustable declination and getting comfortable using it will pay off.

   Take care to get your compass readings as accurate as possible. It's a little easier with a mirror compass, as you can view both the object and the compass vial at the same time. With a simple baseplate compass, you'll have to point it carefully at the object before rotating the vial. Keeping the compass level will let the magnetic needle rotate freely.

   As shown in the diagram on page 122, the uncertainty in your position increases the farther you are from the reference object. If you can only measure an object's bearing to within 5 degrees, the uncertainty in your position will be 450 feet per mile. If the object is a mountain peak 10 miles away, your uncertainty is 4500 feet— nearly a mile. By improving the accuracy of your measurements to

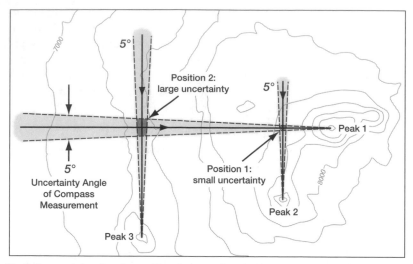

The farther you are from the reference object, the greater the uncertainty in your position. At Position 1, the reference objects are nearby and the uncertainty is small. At Position 2, the uncertainty is larger, especially because you are far from Peak 1.

2 degrees, the uncertainty drops to only 180 feet per mile—a good reason to measure bearings as accurately as possible.

With two people, you can improve the accuracy of measurements taken with a simple baseplate compass. One person kneels down, holds the compass at eye level (keeping it level), and points it at the object. The other person remains standing to view the compass vial. This person carefully rotates the vial to center the compass needle inside the north reference indicator while the kneeling person keeps the compass level and pointed at the object.

3. Correct the measured bearings for magnetic declination, if necessary.

4. For each object, draw a line on the map through the object at the bearing angle you measured to it. This line is known as a position line. You know that you must be somewhere along this line.

In this situation, the bearings you measured are from your unknown position to the known object—the opposite of the situation described in Chapter 3, where you knew your current position but not your destination. In this case, after setting the correct bearing on the vial, lay the compass on the map so the direction-of-travel arrow points in the direction of the object. The front edge of the compass should be touching it, as shown in the illustration. Now adjust the entire compass (don't turn the vial!) so that 0° points to the top of the

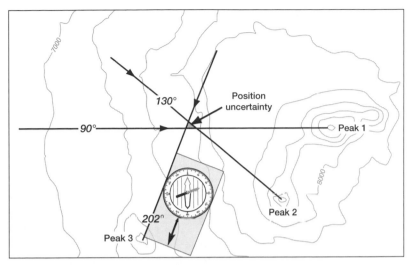

To triangulate your position, plot the bearings you have measured from your current position to at least two (preferably three) objects you have identified on the map. Notice that with three objects, the lines probably won't all intersect at the same spot. You are most likely somewhere within the triangle of uncertainty.

map, while the front edge of the compass remains in contact with the object. (Don't worry about where the magnetic needle points.) Some compasses include north-south orienting lines to make this job a little easier.

Using a pencil, draw a line along the edge of the compass from the known object toward your location. If the distance is farther than the length of the compass, use a straightedge to extend it. In the unlikely event that you've brought along a ruler for this purpose, that's great. Otherwise, find something else long and straight—the edge of a book or map, for instance. You can also make your own straightedge by folding a sheet of paper in half or tightly stretching a piece of string or fishing line.

5. If you took bearings to two or more objects, your position is where the lines intersect. If you took only one bearing and used a known feature like a river

To read the bearing of an object with a mirror compass, aim the notch on top of the lid at the object so the line down the center of the mirror runs through the apparent center of the vial. Rotate the vial while watching it in the mirror until the north reference indicator aligns with the magnetic needle.

as a handrail, your position is where the bearing line intersects the handrail.

Triangulation is a reasonably accurate way to find your position, though it's not perfect. You'll quickly discover this if you take bearings to more than two objects and plot all the position lines on the map. It's unlikely they'll all intersect at the same spot, but if you've made careful measurements, they should be close. The distance between the various intersections is a good approximation of the error in your measurements.

Dead Reckoning

Suppose you can't spot any identifiable features in the landscape—there's nothing but forest or unbroken swampland, for instance, or perhaps it's foggy. Your objective becomes one of navigating in the correct general direction until you can get to a more identifiable area, a process known by mariners as dead reckoning (where "dead" doesn't necessarily reflect on the fate of its user, but rather is short for "deduced").

Here is where you need to stop and think. If you can estimate how far you have traveled and what direction you have been moving, you can get a rough idea of where you are from your starting point.

Estimating the distance traveled. Your first task is to estimate the distance you have traveled. If you have been hiking, you can apply some general guidelines (for other modes of transportation you'll have to make your own estimates), but every situation is different. A young athlete with only a water bottle will move significantly faster than a 50-year-old office manager carrying a 40-pound pack.

With that caution in mind, here is a simplified, two-step approach: First estimate your average speed and then estimate how long you have been traveling. Knowing these two things, you can estimate the distance you have covered. In this simplified approach, assume you can travel at a standard speed on level ground. Then adjust that rate to account for terrain that requires climbing or descending, and adjust further for the type of terrain. This simplified approach does not account for fatigue.

The following guidelines provide a starting point for estimating walking speeds. (Don't hesitate to modify the numbers to account for your own hiking style.)

▶ On level ground and average terrain, figure you can walk about 2 miles per hour when carrying a moderate pack up to about 30 pounds.

▶ For every 200 feet per mile of elevation gain, deduct 0.3 mile per hour.

▶ For every 200 feet per mile of elevation drop, deduct 0.1 mile per hour.

▶ When walking over soft sand or loose rock, cut the calculated speed in half.

These guidelines apply for elevation gains or losses up to about 800 feet per mile (17 percent grade). Beyond that, you're on your own.

Let's look at an example: Suppose you are hiking a trail that climbs 400 feet in 1 mile. Your approximate speed is therefore 2 miles per hour, minus 0.3 × 2, or 1.4 miles per hour. If your journey was over soft sand, cut the number in half, to 0.7 mile per hour. Of course, these are only generalizations; your mileage may vary. Doing a few hikes in controlled conditions will help you calibrate your normal speed.

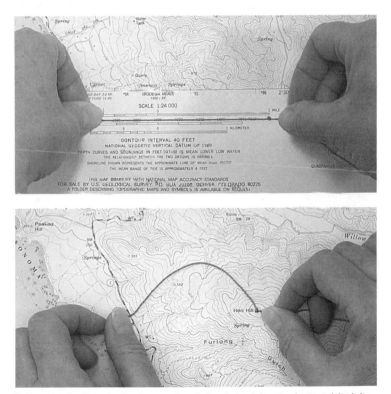

To determine the change in elevation per mile, calculate the total elevation change and divide by the total distance traveled. You can measure distance by laying a string along your approximate path, then calibrating it against the map scale. A knot at one end of the string makes the measurement easier. In this example, the total elevation change is 800 feet and the total distance is 1.5 miles, so the climb is about 500 feet per mile.

Estimating elevation change. You now know how to estimate your speed, but how do you determine the amount of elevation gain or loss? The easiest way is to use your topo map and a piece of string. You first need to calibrate the string using the scale at the bottom of the map. Stretch the string between your thumbs so they are exactly a scale mile apart. Then, holding the string tightly, arrange it to align with your approximate route. Read the elevation contours at your starting and ending points. The difference is the elevation gain or loss in 1 mile. If you've traveled more than a mile, divide the total elevation change by the total distance, or take several mile-long readings along your path and use the average.

Estimating your location. Now you have an estimate of your speed and how long you have been hiking. Multiply your speed by your travel time to get the distance traveled. Here's an example: You've been out for six hours. You estimate you've been climbing at a rate of 400 feet per mile over average terrain, so your hiking speed has been 1.4 miles per hour. Multiply 1.4 miles per hour by six hours to get a total distance of 8.4 miles. You'd probably want to reduce that a bit to account for fatigue and the occasional rest stop you took along the way.

Finally, draw a line on the map from your starting point in the general direction you estimate you've been heading. You are most likely somewhere along this line. If you had been hiking in a straight line the entire time, you would be about 7 to 8 miles away, but that's not usually the case. Here is where you have to apply some judgment and estimate how your actual course came into play. Again, you can use a string that you've calibrated to be about 8 scale miles long. Arrange it in what you believe to roughly approximate your true course to get an idea of where you are.

Altimeter Navigation

Before the advent of GPS, navigation by barometric altimeter was a fairly well-known, though infrequently used, backup method. These days, you don't hear much about it. But you can still use it to advantage—if you remembered to pack a barometric altimeter. I'm not talking about the one you might have in your fancy, high-end GPS receiver. If its batteries have run down or you've lost it over a cliff, its internal altimeter will be no more useful to you than its GPS functions. For this approach to work, you need a separate, backup altimeter.

Altimeters come in two varieties: mechanical units with analog dials and electronic units with digital displays. For years, Thommen (www. thommen.aero) was the premier manufacturer of precision analog altimeters, but they discontinued production in 2008. You can still occasionally find new units for sale on the Internet, and good used units regularly come onto the market. Brunton (www.brunton.com) makes an inexpensive analog altimeter, the ADC Ridge, and a fine digital unit, the ADC Summit, which doubles as a wind-speed indicator and thermometer. You can also find reasonably good digital altimeters on some high-end watches designed for outdoor adventurers. Digital units usually provide higher-resolution readouts, often calibrated to display differences of only a

The Thommen Classic is an example of a precision mechanical altimeter. (Courtesy of Revue Thommen AG)

few feet. Analog units generally are calibrated in 20- to 100-foot increments, although you can do a pretty good job of eyeballing intermediate values. Remember, there is a difference between readout resolution and true accuracy. Given that you won't usually be able to calibrate your altimeter to better than 20-foot accuracy anyway, the resolution of a good mechanical unit is more than adequate.

Before you start using a barometric altimeter, you need to understand a little about how it works. As its name implies, it doesn't directly measure elevation, but rather barometric pressure. Since barometric pressure decreases in a predictable way as you gain elevation, it is possible for the altimeter to give a readout of elevation.

As is usually the case with such matters, it isn't as simple as it first sounds. Barometric pressure is not constant, but changes depending on the weather, which is why a barometer is useful as a weather forecasting tool. Before you can take accurate elevation readings, you first have to perform a calibration. You do this by going to a known elevation—a trailhead, visitors center, or any other location where the elevation is either posted or can be determined from your topo map—and adjusting your altimeter to read that elevation. The closer you are to the elevations you plan to hike, the better. Avoid calibrating your altimeter at sea level when you plan to be hiking at 8000 feet.

Over the course of a day, barometric pressure changes with the weather, causing your apparent elevation to change even if you are standing still. But the effect is less than you might think. If the weather is changing, you may see your apparent elevation change by as much as 100 feet over the course of a few hours. Usually, the change is much less. Changes in temperature can also introduce large errors, particularly with an inexpensive altimeter that doesn't include a temperature compensator. Even if it does, it's never a good idea to keep your altimeter in a warm vest pocket, then take it out and try to make an accurate elevation reading in near freezing temperatures.

You can help compensate for these errors by periodically recalibrating over the course of the day when you reach points of known elevation. These don't need to be places where thoughtful rangers have posted elevation signs. As you hike, look for points you can identify on the map: things like trail junctions or locations where a stream intersects the trail. Then check your topo map. You can get a pretty good idea of your elevation by studying the contour lines around your known location. If your altimeter no longer matches, reset it.

In general, you shouldn't use the elevation readout from your GPS receiver to calibrate a barometric altimeter. GPS elevations are significantly less accurate than GPS horizontal positions. You're better off calibrating your altimeter from your topo map.

Now that you know how to calibrate an altimeter, let's see how to use it in navigation. Basically, knowing your elevation gives you a handrail. On the topo map, you know you are somewhere along a line representing your measured elevation. If you can find the bearing to only one object on the map, your location will be the intersection of that bearing with the line of known elevation.

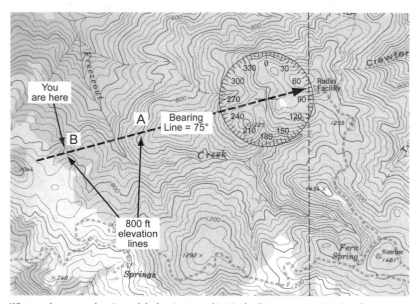

When you know your elevation and the bearing to an object in the distance, your position is at the intersection of the bearing line and your elevation.

Refer to the illustration on the facing page for an example. Suppose you have been cross-country hiking in the area around Freezeout Creek when the batteries in your GPS receiver fail. As you look around, you can see only one recognizable feature, a radio tower toward the northeast. Thankfully, you brought along your altimeter and remembered to calibrate it before you left. You take a reading and find your elevation is 800 feet. Next, you take a compass bearing to the radio tower and find it is at a true bearing of 75° (remember to correct for declination if you haven't adjusted your compass for the local declination).

Pull out your topo map, find the radio tower, and use your compass to plot a bearing line through it at 75°. Remember that this is the bearing from your current position to the radio tower, so you have to be somewhere to the southwest, along the elevation contour of 800 feet.

Notice that the 800-foot contour line intersects the bearing line on either side of Freezeout Creek—once on the downslope and once on the upslope. With a little thought, you realize your immediate terrain slopes downward in the direction of the tower, so you must be at the more westerly intersection.

Identifying Your Destination

Now that you know where you are, you're well on your way to getting back. Remember once again the cardinal rule of GPS navigation introduced in Chapter 1: *It doesn't do you any good to know where you are if you don't know where you want to go.* Even without a working GPS receiver, that's important to remember. Now it's time to figure out your destination.

Often this will be easy. You want to get back to where you started. But if it's getting dark or you are injured you may just want to find the quickest way to civilization. Check your map for promising nearby features. You may be much closer to a paved highway than to your vehicle parked along a lonely Forest Service road. If there's little hope of getting out today, look for a likely spot to spend the night: a ski hut, abandoned ranch house, or perhaps a sheltered cove with a natural spring you can use for drinking water.

Once you've decided on your destination, mark it on the map with a big "X." That way, in the heat of the moment, you're less likely to get confused and start heading toward the wrong objective.

Planning the Route

Now it's time to plan the route to your destination. Even if you intend to go back where you started, you might not want to travel the same route you took out. With a working GPS receiver, you didn't have to worry about the exact route to a destination; your receiver was always updating your bearing. Now, with just a map and compass, you probably want to simplify things.

Unless you're really close to your destination, you probably won't be able to get to it in a straight shot. Just as you use GPS waypoints to create multileg routes, you'll probably need to identify several intermediate destinations—things like stream crossings, ridge lines, trails, or artificial features like radio towers. Make sure these are features you can readily identify when you arrive at them. You don't want to compound your problems by blindly hiking past your goal because you didn't recognize it when you got there.

At this point, you have identified where you are, where you want to go, and intermediate points along the way. You have one more thing to do before you begin hiking: You need to measure the compass bearing and estimate the distance from each intermediate destination to the next.

Follow the same process described more thoroughly in Chapter 3. Start with the bearing from your present position to your first intermediate goal. Lay the compass on the map with its direction-of-travel arrow pointing toward the first goal, then rotate the compass vial so that 0° points straight up (don't worry about where the magnetic needle points). Use the vial's north-south orienting lines, if it has them, as alignment aids. Then read the bearing as the number where the vial meets the bearing indicator. Now estimate the distance between points using the map scale and a piece of string. Write the bearing and distance on the map so you don't forget it. Repeat the process for each intermediate leg. Once you've done this, you're ready to roll.

Following the Route

The first thing to do is go back and read the section about following a bearing, on page 54 in Chapter 3. Many of the same principles apply here. Foremost is the caution against blindly trying to follow a straight line to your destination. Also remember the concept of navigating by visible reference points you've selected in the distance. Don't forget to triangulate your position occasionally as you travel, and update it on the map. And use the methods for estimating travel time on pages 124 and 125 to help determine when you should be approaching a destination.

Aiming Off

Although there are many similarities, navigating a route by map and compass alone is a little different than using a GPS receiver. With GPS, you aren't as concerned about following a precise path because your receiver is constantly updating your bearing. With only a map and compass, you're not so fortunate. Once you unknowingly get off track, there is no easy way to self-correct. And you will get off track; in the wilderness, it isn't easy to navigate a precise bearing over any appreciable distance.

Experienced navigators compensate for this gap using a technique known as "aiming off," a simple concept. Let's say your objective is the one passable crossing of an otherwise dangerous river. From the map, you see the bearing to this crossing is 115°. If you try to follow that exact bearing, you will inevitably miss your objective, but you won't know which direction you are off. When you reach the river, do you turn right or left to find the crossing?

The question is more easily answered if you deliberately navigated slightly off course, say, to the left of the true bearing. When you reach the river, you might not know exactly how far it is to the crossing, but at least you'll know you need to turn right. How much should you aim off? There's no standard answer, but 10 degrees left or 10 degrees right is a good starting point. Decide whether to navigate right or left after studying the map to see which direction has the less hostile terrain.

Aiming off doesn't work so well if your destination isn't located along a suitable handrail like a river or trail. With a calibrated altimeter, you can still attempt the technique by using elevation as a handrail, but remember that you can probably only determine your elevation to an

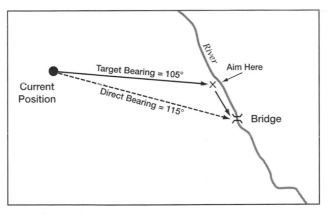

Concept of aiming off

accuracy of 40 or 50 feet. In this case, you will want a destination that is readily visible, even when you can only get within the general area.

Navigating Around Obstacles

Another thing you'll want to know is how to navigate around unforeseen obstacles. Even a 7.5-minute USGS quad with a 40-foot contour interval doesn't show every potential obstacle. A ridge that looked inconsequential on the map might be insurmountable in real life. Or a normally placid creek might be swollen from recent rains. Either way, you need to take a detour, then get back on course.

Here's how to do it: When you come to an obstacle, determine the angle necessary to deviate around it. Navigate this new bearing for a specific amount of time, then reverse your bearing for the same amount of time. If you've done everything right, you will be back on your original course and can return to your original bearing.

Let's look at an example: Suppose you are following a bearing of 100° when you hit an ephemeral lake created by melting spring snow. You have no choice; you have to go around it. After studying the terrain, you decide to alter your course 45° to the left. Your new bearing is then 100° minus 45°, or 55°. Set this bearing on your compass and hike until you are sure you are past the apex of the obstacle. Keep careful track of how long you are traveling on this course deviation.

To determine the bearing necessary to get back to your original course, calculate the complementary bearing: 100° plus 45°, or 145°. Assuming you're on similar terrain, hike this bearing for the same amount of time, and you should be back in line with your original track. If the ter-

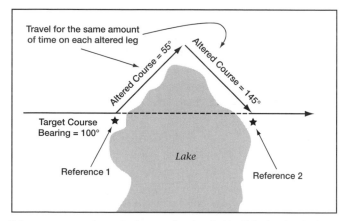

To improve accuracy when navigating around an obstacle, identify landmarks at both near and far sides of the obstacle (in this case a lake) to use as references. When you reach the far side, sight from 2 back to 1 to confirm you are again on track.

rain is substantially different—say, one leg is downhill and the other is uphill—use the method for estimating travel speed described earlier in this chapter to determine when you have covered the equivalent distance. You can now set your compass back to 100° and continue on course.

A second example illustrates another thing to consider about compass bearings: how to deal with math that crosses through a bearing of 0° or 360°. Suppose you are navigating a bearing of 40° when you come to a swollen river perpendicular to your path. You know your best bet for a safe crossing is to your left, so you need to adjust your compass bearing left by 90°. Your new bearing is 40° minus 90°, or -50°. Search as you might, you won't find a bearing of *negative* 50° anywhere on your compass. Whenever you end up with a negative bearing, you must subtract that number from 360°. In this case, your bearing is 360° minus 50°, or 310°.

Similarly, if you were hiking a bearing of 310° and needed to turn 90° to the right, your calculated bearing would be 310° plus 90°, or 400°. Whenever this number is larger than 360°, you must subtract 360° from it. So your new bearing would be 400° minus 360°, or 40°.

Many other tricks of the trade used by skilled map-and-compass navigators are beyond the scope of this book. If you want to learn more, check out the sources listed in Appendix II. But if not, don't worry. The concepts covered in this chapter should be enough to get you out of difficulty when your GPS receiver fails. Just remember they won't work if you haven't bothered to pack a map and compass.

Primitive Navigation Techniques

E ven if you're diligent about preparing for disaster, there may come a time when you face a more difficult situation. You're deep in the wilderness, your GPS receiver is lost or broken, and you don't have a map or a compass. Perhaps a bag got lost overboard on a canoe trip, or you've been separated from a companion who had all the navigation gear. Now what do you do?

The first thing to do is to sit down and catch your breath. Don't let panic set in. Remember that generations of adventurers—Daniel Boone, Davy Crockett, and countless other mountain men—traveled regularly through virgin wilderness without so much as map and compass, let alone a GPS receiver. If they could do it, there's hope for you.

You first have to decide whether it's more sensible to try to find your way out, or whether you should sit and wait for a rescue party. If you've been separated from a group or if you told someone of your plans and your expected return, you will probably be better off sitting and waiting, especially if you're injured or disoriented. Rescue teams lament the all-too-frequent story of a lost hiker continuing to wander like a moving target, almost as if he were deliberately avoiding rescue. Search efforts are conducted in a planned way, so if the hiker wanders from an area that hasn't been searched into one that already has, his chances of being found alive diminish considerably.

Once you have decided to wait, there are a few things to keep in mind that will aid your rescue. Rather than continuing to wander, put your energy into two efforts: finding suitable shelter and making yourself obvious to the search team. That way, you're more likely to still be alive when you're eventually found.

Plan for the night well in advance. If the weather is bad, seek shelter under trees or rock alcoves. If you've got matches (always carry waterproof matches in the wilderness), start a signal fire. Even if people aren't yet looking for you, billowing smoke in a wilderness area may be spotted by a fire lookout or reported to authorities by others in the area.

The fire's heat will also keep you warm during the long night. Just be careful about keeping the fire under control, or you could suddenly find yourself in an even worse situation.

Self-Rescue

If you know a search team won't be dispatched, or if your party includes a seriously injured member who needs urgent attention, you may decide it's better to find your own way out. Without map or compass, the task is more challenging, but not impossible. As you learned in the last chapter, there are four steps to the process: determining where you are, deciding where you want to go, picking the route, and following it to your destination.

At this point, most books tell you how to figure out where north is when you don't have a compass. I'll do that in a moment. But finding north solves only part of the problem. Similar to the cardinal rule of GPS navigation, there is what I call a more general cardinal rule of navigation: *It doesn't do you any good to know which direction is north if you don't know which direction you want to travel.*

So before you spend time finding north, ask and answer these three questions:

1. Where am I?

2. Where do I want to go?

3. What direction do I need to go to get there?

Answering the first question may seem impossible. Your initial reaction might be, "If I knew where I was, I wouldn't be lost." But with a little thought, you should be able to come up with at least a general idea.

There may be times when it doesn't really matter. Hike for a few hours in any direction, and you're sure to hit some sort of civilization. If so, that's great. You don't need to know the techniques described here. But sometimes you will be in a situation in which hiking in most directions will only carry you deeper into the wilderness. There might be only one direction that gets you back to civilization, and that's the one you need to follow.

If you have no idea where you are and have decided to find your own way out rather than wait for rescue, one approach is to follow a stream or river in the direction it flows. It should eventually reach a larger river or lake, where you have a better chance of finding civilization. You can also get a sense of direction by looking for commercial aircraft flying high overhead. Sailors have been known to travel the Pacific from California to Hawaii by simply following their contrails.

Another alternative is to scan the night sky for the telltale glow of habitation. But make sure you aren't fooled by a rising or setting moon. Mark the direction on the ground and wait for morning when it is safe to travel. (Night travel is generally not advised except in desert regions when the heat of the day makes travel impractical.)

If these approaches don't work, you'll need to gather your thoughts and list what you do know. The situation is similar to the discussion of dead reckoning in Chapter 9. All you may believe is that you've generally hiked in a northwesterly direction for about seven hours, but even that's enough to get started. At least you then know that hiking southeast for a similar amount of time should get you in the vicinity of your starting point.

The techniques described here show you ways to roughly identify a specific direction, not just north. Some methods give you south, east, or west. Those probably won't be any of the directions you want to head, but once you know a specific direction, you can sketch out a compass rose like the one shown on page 39 in Chapter 3 to find the direction you want to travel.

A couple of words of caution: These methods work in the temperate latitudes of the northern hemisphere. Methods for finding direction in the tropics or southern hemisphere are beyond the scope of this book. Even though none of these techniques gives you the ability to navigate with pinpoint accuracy, they might get you within earshot of a road or visual range of a small town.

Celestial Navigation Techniques

Celestial navigation has been practiced for centuries by mariners sailing the world's oceans. Some of their tried-and-true methods are easily adapted for emergency use on land. These methods don't require the use of elaborate tables or complicated mathematics, neither of which is likely to be practical if you're lost in the wilderness.

Polaris. By far the most accurate method of finding direction without a compass is to use the stars. In Mexico, the U.S., and more northerly latitudes, the North Star, Polaris, is the easiest to identify. Polaris lies almost exactly due north, so close you can use it to determine magnetic declination. The easiest way to find Polaris is to first identify the Big Dipper. As shown in the diagram on page 138, the top of the Dipper points almost directly to Polaris.

In the late fall and early winter, the Big Dipper is low or even below the northern horizon in the evening, making it difficult or impossible to spot. At this time of year, the constellation Cassiopeia, looking

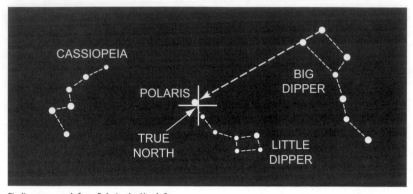

Finding true north from Polaris, the North Star

something like an upside-down "W," is a better reference. The top of the "W" points in the general direction of Polaris.

Orion. Another constellation many people can identify is Orion. The three stars of Orion's belt comprise one of the night sky's most notable features. Orion lies along the celestial equator— no matter where you are, it essentially rises due east and sets due west. If you have a reasonable view of the horizon, you can see where it rises or sets and deduce the appropriate direction.

From about August through December, it's easiest to watch Orion as it rises in the east. In August, it rises in the early morning, between about 3 A.M. and 5 A.M., depending on your location. In December, it rises between 6 P.M. and 8 P.M. From late winter through late spring, it's easier to watch it setting in the west. The middle of summer is problematic because it rises after sunrise and sets before sunset. At that time of the year, you would need to use other stars along the celestial equator as your reference, but that's beyond the scope of this book.

The main problem with celestial navigation on land is that your references are only visible at night. You don't want to be tramping through unknown wilderness in the dark, so the best thing to do is mark the measured direction on the ground in some way—a line in the dirt or a series of rocks, for example. Then wait until morning to start moving.

Directions from the Sun

There are several approaches to measuring direction from the sun. Some are reasonably accurate, others are not. Here are three techniques, in rough order of accuracy.

Sun's Bearing at Noon

This approach can be quite accurate, if performed carefully. The principle is simple: By definition, the sun faces directly south at local noon. With the advent of accurate, quartz crystal-controlled watches, it's relatively easy to determine when it's noon. South is simply the direction to the sun at that instant.

The apparent position of the sun changes most rapidly in the hours around noon, so if you want to be accurate, you need to determine precisely when local noon occurs. The sun moves through an arc of 15 degrees every hour, or 1 degree for every four minutes of time. To find south to within 2 degrees, you need to take the reading within eight minutes of local noon.

During the months of daylight savings time, the largest potential source of error is forgetting to account for the time change. To figure out how to make the adjustment, remember the old saying, "Spring forward, fall back." During daylight savings, clocks are moved forward one hour, so when the clock reads noon, it's really only 11 A.M. standard time. At this time of year, you need to take the reading at 1 P.M., not noon, local time.

Throughout this discussion, I've been using the term local time for good reason. Ever since the late 1800s, the world has been divided into 24 time zones, originally driven by the railroads' need for consistent time at all stations along their routes. Each time zone is 15 degrees wide, and the "standard time" anywhere within a zone is the same. The current time in each successive zone differs by exactly one hour (it's no accident that the sun also moves through a 15-degree arc each hour).

The sun, however, is not due south everywhere in the time zone at the same instant. Only at the longitude line down the center of a zone (the central meridian) is it due south at noon. East of that meridian, the sun is due south earlier than noon; west of it, it's later. "Local noon" is simply defined as the time at which the sun is due south for your current location.

If you're at either edge of a time zone, local noon differs from standard noon by 30 minutes. At the eastern edge, local noon occurs at a standard time of 11:30 A.M. At the western edge, local noon occurs at a standard time of 12:30 P.M. In between, local noon varies depending on how far you are from the central meridian.

If you don't correct for this difference, the direction you determine for due south can be off by 7 degrees or more. Combine that with the fact your watch is probably not perfectly accurate, and your measurement can be off by more than 10 degrees.

Correcting for local time is quite easy, as long as you know your approximate longitude. Find the difference between your current longitude and the central meridian of your time zone. Then apply the rule of four minutes time difference for each degree of longitude difference. Remember that if you're east of the central meridian, noon comes earlier than standard time, and if you're west it comes later. In the U.S., the central meridians for each time zone are the following:

> Eastern time zone: 75° west longitude
> Central time zone: 90° west longitude
> Mountain time zone: 105° west longitude
> Pacific time zone: 120° west longitude

Here's an example: I'm writing this in Santa Rosa, California, located north of San Francisco in the Pacific time zone at longitude 122° 39′ W, which is 2° 39′ west of the central meridian for this zone. Round this to 2.5° and apply the rule of four minutes time difference for every degree of longitude to get a difference of 10 minutes. Since I'm west of the central meridian, local noon occurs at 12:10 P.M. Pacific Standard Time, or 1:10 P.M. Pacific Daylight Time.

A few other minor errors arise because the earth's orbit around the sun is not a perfect circle and its axis of rotation is tilted in relation to its orbit. These can account for another 2- to 3-degree error in your measurement. Considering that without map or compass, your ability to

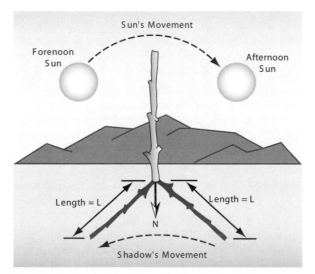

Equal height method for determining north: When the length of the shadow after noon equals the length of the shadow before noon, north is halfway between the two directions.

navigate a precise bearing is rather limited anyway, I wouldn't worry about trying to eke out the last degree or two of accuracy in your measurement.

You can slightly improve the accuracy of this technique by sticking a tall, straight pole or stick vertically into level ground and noting the direction of its shadow at local noon. It will point due north.

Equal Height Method

This method is based on the simple fact that the length of a shadow cast by an object such as a stick a certain number of minutes before noon is the same as its length an equal number of minutes after noon. With this method, you don't need to worry about correcting for your longitude, and you don't even need to know exactly when local noon occurs.

You first need to plant an object like a stick, hiking staff, or ski pole into the ground. The surface of the ground must be as level as possible and the stick as close to true vertical as you can make it. At least 30 minutes before local noon, measure the length of the shadow. Lacking a tape measure, use your belt, some fishing line, or even a fallen tree branch to make the measurement. As you do this, draw a line on the ground to mark the direction of the shadow.

As time progresses, the shadow will get shorter for a time, then begin to lengthen. (If the shadow doesn't get shorter but continues to grow after your initial measurement, you might as well stop, as you've already missed local noon.) Keep measuring the length of the shadow as it grows until it reaches the same length you measured before noon. Immediately draw a new line marking the new direction. North is at an angle halfway between the two lines.

Using Your Watch as a Compass

Despite wide press coverage, this popular technique isn't very accurate. It's based on the somewhat dubious premise that the sun is directly east at 6 A.M., is directly west at 6 P.M., and is due south at noon. Assuming that to be true, then you should be able to use your analog watch to find south. (If you wear a digital watch, you're out of luck.)

Here is the procedure: Align your watch so the hour hand is pointed at the sun. You can do this easily by holding the watch level and placing a slender stick like a match or toothpick vertically in the ground. Align your watch so the shadow falls directly in line with the hour hand. South is then halfway between 12:00 and the current position of the hour hand.

Recalling the previous discussion, you should immediately recognize several problems with this approach. First, it doesn't correct for daylight savings time, so during the summer months you are immediately in error by anywhere between 7 degrees and 23 degrees. Neither does it take into account errors due to the difference in local noon from standard noon, or inaccuracies in your watch. The combination of these errors, even if you've corrected for daylight savings time, can exceed 20 degrees, relegating this approach to last place on the list.

Other methods are often reported in the literature. If you observe the direction of the sun at sunrise or sunset, you can get a rough approximation of east or west. To get accurate results, though, you need to apply a correction factor from a complicated table that you're not likely to have in your pocket.

Another common but inaccurate method is to place a stick vertically in the ground and watch the direction the shadow moves. This gives you a rough indication of east. But because the sun describes an arc as it moves, the direction is only approximate. Don't expect an accuracy of better than 20 degrees using this technique.

Navigating a Bearing Without a Compass

After you've determined what direction you want to go and where north is, you're ready to start your journey. The trick is to navigate that bearing without a compass. The lines you drew in the ground to mark north will be of no help when you're a mile away. And without a reference, most people can't walk a straight line for any distance.

A detailed discussion of the subject is beyond the scope of this book, but here's a tip you may find useful: It's based on the same common-sense approach to navigation described in Chapter 3, with an additional twist. Pick a point in the distance such as a mountain peak or distinctive tree in the direction you want to travel, and use it as a target. Your initial goal is to hike to that target. Now turn around and pick another object directly behind you to serve as a rear anchor point. It doesn't need to be far away; it can be right nearby. It just needs to be something you'll still be able to see when you reach your first target.

Now imagine a tightrope stretched between this rear anchor point and the target object in front of you. You are the tightrope walker. Your goal is to stay on the tightrope as you walk.

In general, you won't always be able to do this. Undoubtedly, you will have to go around obstacles as you hike. Make a point of getting back on the tightrope after you have gone around an obstacle.

You might wonder why you need to worry about tracking a rear anchor point. As long as you can get to your target, why should you care about anything behind you? The problem is that your initial target probably isn't your final goal. When you reach it, you'll need to pick a new target object ahead of you along the same bearing. But since you don't have a compass, how do you know what direction that is?

You could, of course, again use the primitive direction-finding methods described earlier this chapter, but there is an easier way. Look to the rear and locate your anchor point. Now visualize an imaginary line running from it through your current position and continuing forward. Pick a new target along this bearing and continue navigating. You may also need to pick a new anchor point. Continue going, selecting new targets and anchor points as you need them, until you eventually make it back to civilization.

When you don't have a map or compass, knowing how to navigate by visually tracking your surroundings can be the difference between getting to safety and finding yourself farther afield in unknown territory. The time to practice these skills is when you still have a working GPS receiver, not after it's already broken. Whenever you are out with your receiver, consider using the techniques described here to hone your skills in visual navigation.

Part IV
Getting the Most from GPS

Key Concepts

- ▶ All about geocaching

- ▶ Fun things to do with GPS

- ▶ All about track logs

- ▶ How to create accurate trail maps using GPS

- ▶ Using your GPS receiver for highway navigation

- ▶ How to choose a GPS receiver

- ▶ Guide to receivers from popular manufacturers

- ▶ Essential GPS accessories

11

Geocaching

The fast-growing sport geocaching is a great way to practice GPS navigation skills. The concept is simple: One person hides a container, or cache, which typically includes a log book, instruction sheet, and a few trading items, and posts its latitude and longitude coordinates on a website. Other people look up the coordinates of the cache (pronounced *cash*) on the web and then use their GPS receivers to try to find it. When they do, they sign the log book and, if they want, take an item. According to geocaching etiquette, if you take an item you must leave another item to replace it. When you're finished, return the cache to its hiding place for others to find.

It sounds easier than it is. Remember, your receiver is typically only accurate to about 20 or 30 feet, and the cache is often camouflaged and small. Your receiver will only get you into the general area. It's up to you to search around until you find it.

Geocaching was unheard of before the government turned off Selective Availability (page 4) in 2000. But within days, the first cache was planted in Oregon and the sport was off and running. Now it is a worldwide phenomenon, with caches in nearly 200 countries. Hiding spots range from locations far in the wilderness to downtown urban areas. Geocachers run the gamut from dedicated enthusiasts who hike miles in the backcountry to parents and children who go no farther than the local park.

The first caches were fairly large Army Surplus ammo boxes, but these days, almost any container is used. I've seen fake hollow rocks, magnetic key holders, and just about every kind of plastic or rubber container you can imagine. Hollow logs and rock piles seem to be favorite hiding places. A cache placed in the wilderness need not be well-camouflaged, but in an urban area the biggest challenge is hiding it in a way it won't be found by non-geocachers (called "geomuggles" in geocaching lingo, after the nonmagical "muggles" from the Harry Potter stories).

Most caches are placed on public lands, although with the owner's permission they can be placed on private property. Some government

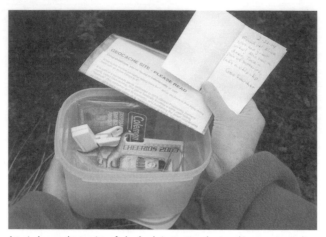

A typical geocache consists of a log book, instruction sheet, and inexpensive trading items housed in a waterproof container.

agencies—viewing geocaches as little more than trash or fearful of potential environmental damage from legions of geocachers tramping willy-nilly over the hillsides—have banned geocaching within their jurisdictions. The National Park Service falls into this category. Other agencies recognize the sport as a way to get more people out to enjoy nature and appreciate their parks. Even public agencies that permit geocaches may require you to get a permit first, so before you hide a cache on public land, make sure you are not in violation of any government regulation.

Typical cache page on www.navicache.com (Courtesy of Navicache.com)

Typical cache page on www.geocaching.com (Courtesy of Groundspeak, Inc.)

GEOCACHING WEBSITES

Before you can find a cache, you need to know where to look. The two most important geocaching Internet sites are www.geocaching.com and www.navicache.com. These sites provide the coordinates for thousands of hidden caches. Both provide free access (after you complete a free registration), although Geocaching.com also offers what they call a premium membership that gives you, for a fee, early notification of new caches and access to otherwise unpublished caches. Navicache.com takes a different approach, based on the premise of complete free access to the site. Both provide many opportunities for a good hunt.

If you prefer to find cache coordinates by way of a map rather than entering zip codes or latitudes and longitudes, check out Buxley's Geocaching Waypoint at www.brillig.com/geocaching. This "search engine" page provides map-based links to the caches on Navicache.com and other web pages (legal issues currently prevent links to the Geocaching.com caches).

An Internet search on the words *geocaching* or *geocache* will turn up hundreds of other websites, including regional and international geocaching organizations, upcoming events, and various words of advice. If you're new to the sport, it might be worthwhile to spend a little time browsing a few such sites to learn more about it.

Cache Types

Geocaching is so new that the rules of the game are still evolving. There are several generally accepted types of caches:

Traditional cache. Also called a "normal cache," this original type of cache includes a log book and prizes in a container roughly the size of a breadbox. Army Surplus ammo boxes were the original favorite containers, but too many people considered the boxes themselves to be neat prizes and carted them away. Now you are more likely to see Rubbermaid containers, old peanut butter jars, or empty paint buckets. Caches placed in containers about the size of a 5-gallon paint can are known as "large caches."

Micro cache. Micro caches are similar to traditional caches but much smaller. Film canisters, magnetic key holders, and empty breath-mint tins are examples. Often there is little room for anything other than a miniature log book.

Offset cache. This is a little more complicated than a traditional cache. The published coordinates direct you to some sort of point of interest. You must then continue to a nearby location based on information you learn at the site or from information given on the cache's web page. See the sidebar on page 154 for more information on finding offset caches.

Multipart caches. Multipart caches require you to find multiple caches to complete your quest. In one version, several caches are posted on the Internet. Each cache you find gives you a piece of information necessary to find a final, unpublished cache. In another version, each successive cache gives you coordinates to the next cache in a sequence.

Virtual cache. In urban or heavily traveled rural areas, it isn't always possible to place a physical cache. The base of Yosemite Falls, for example, sees so many visitors that it would be impossible to keep a cache hidden for long, even if it weren't against park regulations. A virtual cache gives you the coordinates of a particular point of interest and asks you to answer a question about the location. You email the answer to the "owner" of the cache to prove you were there. This cache is the only type permitted in national parks. Virtual caches have become popular enough to warrant their own website at www.waymarking.com.

Reverse cache. Also called a "locationless cache," a reverse cache is the opposite of a traditional one. Instead of going to a specific waypoint to discover what is there, you are instructed to find a specific type of object and record its coordinates. For more information, visit www.waymarking.com. Public playgrounds, murals, coin-operated binoculars, and suspension bridges are a few of the many categories you'll find listed at the site.

Other cache types can include puzzle caches, event caches, earthcaches, and letterbox hybrids. Refer to Geocaching.com or Navicache.com for more information.

Difficulty and Terrain

Caches are rated by their owners in terms of difficulty and terrain using a scale from 1 to 5, with 1 being the easiest and 5 the hardest. Difficulty refers to how hard it is to find the cache, including such factors as the length of the hike and the effort required to find the cache once you get to the general area. Terrain describes the physical nature of the trail to the cache. A rating of 1 indicates the terrain is wheelchair accessible. A rating of 5 indicates a cache that may require specialized equipment such as climbing or scuba gear. Use the ratings as a general guideline. Because they are assigned subjectively by cache owners, there can be considerable difference in scoring from one cache to another.

Geocaching Rules

Geocaching involves several important rules:

1. If you take an item from the cache, leave an item. Check rule 6 below for information on what not to put in a cache.

2. Record your visit in the log book.

3. Put the cache back in the same place you found it, unless its instructions say otherwise.

4. Report your visit on the website where you found the coordinates.

If you plan to hide a cache, some additional considerations include:

5. Include a log book for visitors to record their experiences. If there's room, include a pencil. If not, be sure your online description of the cache tells people to bring their own.

6. Use commonsense when stocking your cache. Never put anything dangerous in it like fireworks, explosives, ammunition, knives or other weapons, alcohol, illegal substances, or pornography. Remember that geocaching is a family sport, and since children are often the first to find a cache, plan accordingly. Food items are also strongly discouraged. Animals are more likely than humans to benefit from such treasures. Besides, would you really want to sample a chocolate

bar that may have sat out in the elements for who knows how many months? If you want to provide food, do so with gift certificates for free hamburgers or ice-cream cones at a local restaurant.

7. Never bury a cache. The sport is based on a premise of minimizing environmental impact, so place it where it can be found with minimal damage to the environment. (It's OK to cover it loosely with leaves or twigs, but never to the point where it is completely hidden from view.)

8. When you place a cache, you become its "owner." You are responsible for visiting it on occasion to make sure it is in good condition and that the area around it doesn't show signs of overuse. Remove a cache if the environmental impact becomes more than minimal. For this reason, you shouldn't place a cache while on vacation or in a remote area you can't visit regularly.

9. Make sure to record the correct GPS coordinates. Use the WGS 84 datum, and in general, use the degrees-decimal minutes format. Turn on averaging, if available in your receiver, to improve the waypoint's accuracy. Check the rules of the specific website you are using for additional information.

Finding a Cache

If you're new to geocaching, you should practice finding caches to learn the general principles of the sport before you start hiding caches of your own. From the home pages at either Navicache.com or Geocaching.com, you can enter a zip code to get a listing of all caches in the immediate area. The sites also have advanced capabilities that allow you to search on latitude-longitude coordinates, cache names, and several other criteria.

The result of your search will be a list of nearby caches, including hyperlinks to the individual cache pages. Click on a link to learn about a specific cache. Here you will see its latitude-longitude coordinates (Geocaching.com also provides UTM coordinates), learn more about the cache, and read the

Sugarloaf Country
by Daffodil [profile]

N 38° 26.312 W 122° 29.969
UTM: 10S E 543681 N 4254591
E 8.5mi from your home coordinates

Click icon to download:
LOC Waypoint File (*.loc)
Read about waypoint downloads

If you don't like to manually enter waypoint coordinates, www.geocaching.com lets you send them directly to your GPS receiver. You may first need to install a software application available from that website. (Courtesy of Groundspeak, Inc.)

log notes recorded by previous visitors. Pick a cache that sounds appealing and enter its coordinates into your receiver. Now you're ready to go find it.

If you don't like to manually enter coordinates, Geocaching.com offers a simpler alternative. On the detail page for each cache, just below the cache coordinates, are buttons that allow you to either send the cache coordinates to a compatible GPS receiver, transfer them to a compatible mobile phone, or store them on your computer as a .LOC file. The "Send to GPS" button works with many receivers from Garmin and DeLorme. Connect your receiver to your computer and click the button. The program automatically detects your receiver and transfers the cache coordinates to it. (It uses the GC code, not the cache name, as the waypoint name.)

If you don't have a compatible receiver you can still transfer cache coordinates, but it is a little more complicated. You must first store the coordinates as a .LOC file on your computer, then use a program such as EasyGPS to transfer the caches to your receiver. Detailed instructions can be found by clicking the "Read About Waypoint Downloads" link just above the download buttons.

Preparation

The web page for a cache defaults to a high-level map of the surrounding area. It might not be detailed enough to show where to start your hunt. You want to avoid starting from a spot that appears close only to find the way blocked by a canyon, housing development, oil refinery, etc. It's a good idea to study a more detailed map before you head out.

Geocaching.com and Navicache.com both give you the option of displaying the cache location on other online maps including TopoZone and MapQuest. Topo maps are a good bet for caches hidden in rural areas. Street maps are best for urban caches. And this is one area where a mapping receiver really shines. With the correct map loaded, your GPS unit can guide you directly from your home to the jumping-off point.

If you're going to a cache that's off the beaten path, prepare the same way you would for any serious hike. Assemble a backpack with a few basic items: GPS receiver, extra batteries (very important!), magnetic compass, water, snacks, first-aid kit, and perhaps a jacket or windbreaker. A cell phone can be handy if you will be within its coverage area, and may work even if you're not. Don't forget to include items you can use to trade. If you plan to be a geocaching regular, you may want to keep the kit together permanently so you can head out at a moment's notice.

FINDING OFFSET CACHES

To find an offset cache, you must first go to the published waypoint coordinates and then perform additional navigation. For example, if you are told that once you reach the waypoint, the cache lies 80 feet away at a bearing of 60°, how do you find it?

Figuring out its direction is fairly easy—use your magnetic compass. Knowing how far to walk is more difficult. Some Garmin receivers have a feature called PROJECT WAYPOINT that allows you to create a new waypoint at a specified bearing and distance away from a stored waypoint. But even if your receiver doesn't have this feature, you can still use it to find the cache. Here's how: First, determine the back bearing of the cache. This is the bearing you would use to walk from the cache back to the published waypoint. If the cache's bearing is less than 180°, find the back bearing by adding 180° to it; if it is greater than 180°, subtract 180°. For instance, if the cache's bearing is 60°, the back bearing would be 240°.

To find the cache, call up the published waypoint, activate the GOTO function, and navigate to it. Once you get there, the cache is 80 feet away at a bearing of 60°. Using your magnetic compass, walk toward the cache, and watch your receiver as the bearing and distance on the screen change. Remember that the bearing you see is the back bearing—the bearing back to the published waypoint—not the bearing to the cache. Keep moving until you are the correct distance and bearing away. In our example, you are at the cache when the published waypoint is 80 feet away from you at a bearing of 240°.

Search

It can be just as challenging to find the right parking spot for your car as it is to find the cache. Some cache web pages will give you an idea of where to start, but in many cases, you're on your own. If you studied a map before you started, you should be able to get reasonably close.

Park your car and turn on your GPS receiver to get a position fix. If the cache is any significant distance away, first mark the location of your car as a waypoint. You don't want to get yourself into the unenviable position of having found the cache but having no idea how to get back. Remember the cardinal rule of GPS navigation: *It doesn't do you any good to know where you are if you don't know where you want to go.*

If you've studied the first two sections of this book, you know how to navigate with a GPS receiver; I won't repeat those instructions here.

If you have any questions, now would be a good time to go back and review the basics, starting on page 37.

Many geocachers keep their GPS receivers turned on for the duration of the quest. That way, they can use the compass page as their primary navigation tool. Ever since the demise of Selective Availability, the compass page has become reasonably useful, even at walking speeds. It's still a good idea to carry a magnetic compass as a backup and for use when you are standing still.

Be sure to check the satellite status page occasionally. If you are navigating through forests or canyons, your receiver could lose its lock on a satellite or two and drop back into 2D mode. If so, your indicated position could be hundreds of feet away from your actual position. Move around as necessary to keep your receiver operating in 3D mode.

The last 15 to 20 feet are the most challenging. At this point, it's best to put your receiver away—it won't be able to help you now. Here is where your search skills become important. Try to imagine where you would have hidden the cache if it were yours. Hollow logs, rock piles, and clumps of brush all make likely hiding spots. The rules of geocaching prohibit buried caches, so don't dig up the ground. But since caches are often loosely covered with twigs, small rocks, or dried grass, look around.

Use commonsense when checking concealed spots. Snakes, spiders, or scorpions could be lurking within; you may want to carry a hiking staff to probe such areas. And always keep an eye out for poison oak, poison ivy, poison sumac, or whatever other poisonous plants are native to the surrounding area.

At the Cache

Once you've spotted the cache and before you retrieve it, look around to see if anyone else is nearby. You don't want a geomuggle to discover and pillage the cache after you've left. Wait until it's safe, then retrieve it. Record your visit in the log, swap items if you want, then seal the cache and replace it where you found it. Don't forget to log your visit on the web page when you return home.

Hiding a Cache

Eventually, after you have found a few caches, you may want to hide your own. Reread the rules for hiding caches on pages 151 and 152, then decide on a plan. At first, you will probably want to keep things simple by hiding a traditional cache. Do some research before hiding it. Are there already other caches nearby? To minimize environmental impact, cache websites usually won't accept new caches placed too close to an existing cache. Also make sure your intended site doesn't violate laws or property rights. Don't place a cache on private property without the owner's permission. On public lands, check with the managing agency if you aren't sure of their geocaching policy. Some agencies require that you get a permit before placing a cache.

You'll also have to decide how difficult you want to make the search. A cache that's easy to reach will be visited more often than one placed far in the wilderness. But the challenge of the find can make the wilderness cache a more rewarding experience for those who attempt it. Also give consideration to how you hide the cache. Don't make people scramble across a delicate natural environment to get to it. The best caches are ones that give the visitor another reason to be there besides the cache—a great scenic view or historical point of interest, for example. Check the website where you plan to post the cache for any additional rules they may have.

Remember, your cache will lie exposed to the weather year-round, so choose a container suitable for the environment. If possible, use a plastic or metal container with an airtight seal. Avoid glass jars since they break easily. Label the container as a geocache according to instructions on the appropriate web page, so that if it's accidentally found by a geomuggle, they won't think it's trash and dispose of it.

You already know what not to put in a cache, but equally important is what to put in. You don't need to spend a lot of money. Cheap toys are great, since many geocachers are children. Other common items include cash (coins or paper), CDs, DVDs, gift certificates, sunscreen, books, or almost anything else you can think of. Use your imagination. Some cache owners include single-use disposable cameras. The idea is for visitors to take their pictures at the cache and leave the camera there. When all the shots are exposed, the cache owner develops the film and posts the photos on the web.

Travel Bugs and Geocoins

A "travel bug" (also called a "hitchhiker") is an item intended to travel from one cache to another. The item can be anything—toys and stuffed animals are favorites—but it is distinguished by a coded metal tag dangling from it. If you take a travel bug from a cache, you're not supposed to keep it, but rather place it in another cache and keep it moving. You also need to log onto the website indicated on the tag to record that you have taken it and to read the instructions the owner has posted for it. The goal might be for the bug to travel around the world or hit as many states as possible in a specific period, so don't hold onto a travel bug

Travel bug (left) and geocoin (right)

for any length of time. As soon as practical, go out to another cache and send it on its way. Then make sure you go to its online log and record where you placed it, so the owner can track its journey.

A geocoin is a custom coin created by an individual or group to be left as a calling card in a geocache. Like a travel bug, a geocoin can have a unique tracking ID, but geocoins are also meant to be kept or traded. When you find a geocoin, be sure to log onto the designated website to see what to do with it. Geocoins have become so popular that numerous companies now create affordable custom coins for geocachers in quantities as small as 100 pieces or less. To learn more, check the Geocoins Information Page at www.geocaching.com/track/geocoin.aspx.

Geocaching can be a great sport for the whole family. Follow the simple guidelines in this chapter, and you will have a good excuse to get outside with your GPS receiver more often.

More Fun and Games

Once you are comfortable with your GPS receiver, you'll undoubtedly want to find new ways to use it, if for no other reason than to justify to your family why you bought it. In this chapter, we'll give you a few ideas for fun things to do with your receiver, starting with solo activities and finishing up with team games. Don't be afraid to use these ideas as starting points to invent your own variations.

Track Log Maps

The previous chapters focused on how to use a GPS receiver to get to a destination. But your receiver also excels at another task—recording the route you took to get there. All receivers designed for the outdoors can generate a track log (called a "trail" by some manufacturers), a detailed record of the path you took to get from a starting point to a destination. You'll often hear it described as a "bread-crumb trail," in reference to the old story of Hansel and Gretel. But unlike poor Hansel's bread

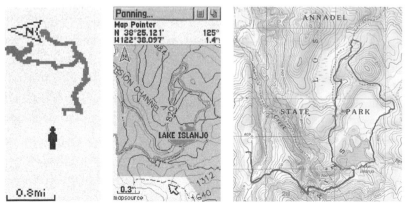

Track logs as displayed on the eTrex (left) and Vista (center). At right, the eTrex track log has been downloaded to a USGS map using TOPO! software. This example clearly shows how some park trails have been relocated from their original routes to reduce environmental impact on sensitive meadows. (Map created with TOPO! © 2006 by National Geographic)

crumbs, which were eaten by birds, your receiver's track log remains in memory until you explicitly delete it.

Track Back Feature

A track log can be valuable in many ways. In the simplest case, you can use it to retrace your exact path back to a starting point. (In contrast, following a waypoint bearing only shows you the straight-line path to a destination.) Simply turn on your receiver, activate the track log feature before you start out, and let your receiver keep track of your path. Every time you pass a threshold in either time or distance from the last log point, another point is automatically added. This process continues until you either complete your journey or the track log memory gets filled. Memories typically range from 1,000 to 10,000 points, so even the smallest memory should be sufficient to record a journey of a few hours or more.

Be sure to clear your receiver's track log memory before you start out, and keep your receiver turned on the entire time you're traveling. That way you'll get a complete record of your path without any extraneous information. When you are ready to return, go to the map page and zoom in enough to get a detailed view of the track. Then simply follow the track back to your origin. Many receivers make the job easier by providing a "track back" feature that creates a route from your track. Your receiver generates a number of phantom waypoints from the stored track log and connects them just like any other route.

Using a Track Log with a Computer

Perhaps more interesting is the fact that a track log allows you to store a complete record of your journey for future reference. Once your receiver has recorded a track log, you can download it to a computer where you can display and analyze it on a software map. This kind of mapping is so useful that all of Chapter 13 is devoted to showing you how to make the most accurate maps. If you don't need that level of accuracy and only want to log a record of your journey, the following paragraphs give you a simplified overview.

To create an accurate track log the receiver must have a clear view of the sky the entire time. This eTrex is mounted to a backpack shoulder strap.

First, for your receiver to capture an uninterrupted log, you must leave it turned on for the entire journey. Make sure your batteries are fresh and always carry spares. Your receiver must also remain locked into the satellites, so don't bury it in a pocket or backpack. Keep it out where it has a clear view of the sky and its antenna is correctly oriented. This is one situation where an external antenna is useful; you can place the receiver in your pocket or backpack and keep only the antenna visible. I've had good success with a Garmin GPSMAP 60CSx and an external antenna.

If you're handy with tools, you can make a custom clip to attach an external antenna to your clothing.

I designed a custom clip so I can easily attach the antenna to my shirt. I've also been successful placing it inside a hat. Tilley (www.tilley.com) makes several hats with a pocket that can hold the antenna inside the crown. I run the cable under my shirt to be less conspicuous.

Another thing to remember is that a track log remains in memory until you explicitly clear it; before you start a new journey, clear any existing data that remains from previous trips. Otherwise, the old and new data will be recorded as a continuous jumble of information. You usually clear the track log from the SETUP page, although on some receivers you do it from the MAP page.

Finally, remember your receiver has a fixed amount of track log memory. In most cases, it takes several hours to fill up, but when it does get filled, your receiver starts overwriting the oldest data with the newest. (Most receivers have an option to stop recording when the memory is full.) The TRACK LOG screen shows you what percentage of the memory has been used.

Some receivers let you store the active track to a separate memory. If your receiver lets you do this, you'll want to store it when the track log memory approaches 100 percent, then start a new log. You can later download all the stored tracks into a computer, where they can be joined and analyzed as a single record. This option isn't available in less expensive receivers that have only a single track log memory. Note that most receivers don't save a stored track at full resolution, so if that's important to you, don't delete it from the active track log.

You can select several options when creating a track log. The most useful is the "automatic" mode, where the receiver decides when your position has changed enough to justify adding another point to the track. It is smart enough to know that if you're driving on the freeway at 60 miles per hour, there can be more distance between points than if you are walking a trail at 2 miles per hour.

You typically have two other options: Store points at either a constant time interval or a specific distance from the previous point. In almost all cases, you are better off leaving your receiver set to automatic mode.

Before you can do anything with the track log, you need to get it out of your receiver and into your computer. For this, you need a software mapping program like those described in Chapter 6. A program like National Geographic TOPO! or MyTopo Terrain Navigator makes it easy to import the track log directly onto a map and see precisely where you have traveled.

Using track logs, you can do such things as chart a river's course or design a marathon route . These are fairly obvious applications, but there are others as well. I have used this approach to accurately record trail routes and distances for my hiking guidebooks. An avid mountain biker friend used his GPS receiver to plot a 40-mile course through a nearby state park. He then rode the course to celebrate his 40th birthday—and swears he'll continue matching distance to age every 10 years until he turns 80!

Geotagging Photos

Many photographers want to record the exact location of every photo they take so they can later sort their photos based on location. With digital photos, it is possible to embed latitude and longitude coordinates along with other geographic information in the digital file, a process called *geotagging*. (Sometimes it's incorrectly called *geocoding*, but *geocoding* refers to the process of determining latitude/longitude coordinates from an address.) Data embedded in a digital file is called *metadata*. It can include such items as the date and time the photo was taken, the camera and lens used, aperture, exposure time, etc. Industry standards for metadata allow for optional data such as latitude-longitude, altitude, and the direction the camera was pointing.

The easiest way to geotag a photo is to use a digital camera that has a built-in GPS receiver. Although still rare at this writing, several are available from such manufacturers as Nikon and Canon. Some cameras allow you to connect an external GPS receiver to automatically geotag photos as they are taken. If your camera uses SDHC memory cards, another option is to buy a special memory card from Eye-Fi (www.eye.fi) that geotags photos as they are taken using a Wi-Fi positioning service from Skyhook Wireless. This feature only works when you are within range of Wi-Fi networks.

If none of these options work for you, the next best thing is to use your GPS receiver. The simplest but most laborious way is to record a GPS waypoint each time you take a photo. Then, when you are back at home, you can manually enter the latitude-longitude coordinates into each file's metadata using a software program such as Photoshop Elements or Adobe Bridge, or with a website such as Flickr (www.flickr.com) or Picasa (http://picasa.google.com).

If you have a digital camera, a somewhat easier method is to leave your GPS receiver turned on so that it records a track log for the entire time you are shooting. A GPS track log not only records where you were, but also the exact time you were there. When you get back home, you can then use a software program that compares the time stamp on the digital photo file with the GPS track log to find your latitude-longitude coordinates at the time you took the picture. The program automatically adds these coordinates to the photo's metadata. For this to work, the clock in your digital camera must be synchronized to GPS time, usually as simple as manually setting your camera's clock to the same time as that on your GPS receiver. Programs that can geotag photos from GPS track log data include Microsoft Pro Photo Tools (www.microsoft.com/prophoto), GeoPhoto (www.ovolab.com/geophoto), and HoudahGeo (www.houdah.com/houdahGeo/index.html).

GPS Golf

A good part of a successful golf game is knowing the correct club to use for the current distance to the green, and a GPS receiver can help you. While you can rent or buy many commercial GPS-based golfing systems, it is possible to use a standard GPS receiver. You first have to store as GPS waypoints the positions of all the greens and any other points of interest (sand traps, water hazards, etc.). Then when you are on the course, simply use the GOTO function to determine your distance from the green or hazard. Remember that most receivers report distance in feet, so you'll have to mentally divide the answer by three to convert it to yards.

The roughly 20-foot accuracy of standard GPS is somewhat marginal for golf. Newer receivers with WAAS capability can reduce the margin to a more acceptable 2 yards or less—if you can lock onto a WAAS signal. Fortunately, most golf courses are fairly wide open spaces, so your chances of picking up a WAAS satellite are better than average.

You might wonder how to create the coordinates of the various waypoints. If you regularly play the same course, you can store the important waypoint locations during one round so you can use them in later rounds. You might also consider trading this information with others who have data for other courses.

Find the Flags

This is a group exercise I often use with students in my GPS navigation classes. It takes a little preparation, but the results are well worth it. It works best for groups of between six and 12 people. You'll need several GPS receivers and access to a fairly large open area such as a state or regional park that doesn't get a lot of traffic. (Make sure you use a park where it is permissible to hide objects for later recovery.)

The concept is fairly straightforward. A day or so before the game, one person—the master of ceremonies—goes into the park and hides a number of objects (I use small flags of the type landscapers use to mark the locations of sprinkler heads), being certain to accurately record their coordinates as GPS waypoints. The master of ceremonies should hide the flags so they are not likely to be discovered accidentally by strangers, while avoiding unwarranted environmental impact or hazards such as poison oak. On the day of the game, the group gathers at the designated meeting spot and the master of ceremonies hands out waypoint coordinates.

It works best if the group is divided into several teams of two or three people each, depending on the number of GPS receivers available. At minimum, one person from each team needs a GPS receiver while the others should at least have magnetic compasses so they can follow the indicated GPS bearings. Each team competes against all the other teams to be the first to find specific flags.

For a group of 12 people, I typically hide 10 flags. The group is organized into four teams of three people each. Each team receives coordinates for two of the 10 flags, plus a sealed envelope containing the coordinates of the final two flags. Each team must program the coordinates into their receivers and go search for their two assigned flags. Only after they have found their assigned flags can a team open the envelope and begin the search for the final two flags, which all teams are competing to find. The first team to find their two assigned flags plus the final two flags is declared the winner.

Depending on skill levels, you can make the game more or less complicated. For novices, you should stick to a common datum and position format for all waypoints. For more skilled groups, you might want to list some waypoints in degrees-minutes-seconds format and others in degrees-decimal minutes format. You might also want to reference some to WGS 84 and others to NAD 27 (or even some exotic datum like Easter Island 1967, as long as you know it works in your region and that everyone's receiver includes it as a choice).

It's best if you can place flags at least 100 feet apart so that everyone isn't stumbling over each other as they search. You'll also want to keep in mind the athletic ability of the individuals. I typically place flags about a quarter to a half mile from the starting point and assign the more athletic members of the group to find the more distant flags. Consider other details, too. The master of ceremonies is responsible for helping any teams that get into difficulty. Inexpensive, two-way radios can be useful communications tools during the hunt and to help the master of ceremonies steer a team in the right direction if they start diverging from their goal. A prize such as a bottle of wine or picnic lunch at the end serves as ample motivation.

GPS Team Building

Here's an exercise I sometimes use with company executives as part of a leadership training program. It is also useful for youth groups or athletic teams who must understand the value of cooperation. In industry, managers must learn that their business will only be successful if two things happen: If each individual department is successful on its own, and if all departments work toward a common goal. This exercise is designed to drive home both of those points.

It is somewhat similar to "Find the Flags." A group of between six and 15 people is divided into several teams of two or three members each. There must be at least one GPS receiver for each team. A reasonably large open space such as a park is also essential. A day or two ahead of time, I hide several objects in the park and record their waypoint coordinates. But instead of hiding flags, I use small plastic containers. The number of containers is one more than the number of teams—if there are three teams, for example, I hide four containers.

The last container is the ultimate goal. It is the objective that everyone is working toward. It might contain a small reward—coupons that can be redeemed for food, drink, or some memento of the program, for instance. Each of the other containers includes two things: the name of a second waypoint location and a clue to the location of the final container. Each team must find their assigned initial container, then go to the second waypoint. There is no hidden treasure at this location; it is just a meeting point. The idea is that all teams converge at this point and piece together the clues to find the last container. Only if each team is successful individually can the entire group reach the final goal.

Keep in mind that if you're doing this with GPS novices, you won't want to take the time to teach them the subtleties of position formats or map datums. It's best if you program all the waypoints into all the receivers ahead of time, then give the teams the waypoint names and teach them how to use the GOTO function. The clues can then simply consist of parts of the final waypoint's name.

I generally keep the instructions somewhat vague. Players learn how to use the GOTO function, and they learn the location of their initial container. But they are on their own to figure out what to do after that. Part of the challenge is figuring out why you are at the second waypoint and what to do when you get there.

Make sure to program the coordinates of every waypoint into every GPS receiver. That way, a team that has successfully found its clue has the option of helping another team that is struggling. Whether or not they think to do that is up to them. I normally wouldn't offer that advice ahead of time but rather let them figure it out for themselves as part of learning to work together. Once again, inexpensive, handheld, two-way radios can be useful tools to help the teams communicate with each other.

Orienteering: GPS Relay Race

Orienteering is a competitive sport in which you find your way as quickly as possible across wilderness terrain to a series of control points using only a map and compass. Although it has traditionally been a solo sport where GPS receivers are expressly prohibited, GPS-based events are becoming more common. Here's a similar, team-oriented idea that relies on GPS skills rather than map-reading skills. It consists of a relay race in which each contestant uses a GPS receiver to navigate to where the next team member is waiting. It is particularly suited to runners, bicyclists, or cross-country skiers. Each participant needs a receiver.

Start with two or more teams of four contestants each. Every contestant needs a GPS receiver. Well in advance of race day, the race organizer must design the course. City streets or backcountry trails work equally well. Unlike true orienteering, no topo map is involved. Instead, contestants are given GPS waypoint coordinates and must use their skill and judgment to find the best route.

In designing the course, consider the type of competition. If it is a footrace, each leg might be a mile or two long. For cyclists, it could be 5 miles or more. Plot a closed-loop course—one that ends where it began. Identify three spots along the way at roughly equal intervals and record these locations as GPS waypoints. These will become the relay exchange points. Don't let any of the participants know these locations ahead of time.

On race day, each member of the team except the first contestant receives the starting and ending coordinates for his or her leg of the race. The starting contestant is given the coordinates for the complete list of waypoints. His GPS receiver will serve as the "baton" that is passed between each relay member. Its track log will prove that it traversed the entire course, so it must be cleared before starting the race.

Prior to the start, team members must individually enter the waypoints for their leg of the race into their receiver. To make it more challenging, these waypoints should not be shared with other team members. Contestants then find their way to the starting points of their own legs, where they will wait for the handoff. Depending on distance and terrain, they may get there by walking, driving, or bicycling as appropriate.

Give the contestants enough time to get into position (15 to 30 minutes should be ample), then start the race. The first contestants must get to the waypoint at the end of their leg by following any route they choose. If all goes well, when they arrive, they will meet the second contestant and exchange GPS receivers. Of course, their success depends on both contestants having accurately programmed the waypoint coordinates and having accurately navigated to the correct position. Assuming a successful transfer, the race continues through all the legs until the final contestant reaches the finish line carrying the GPS receiver that traversed the entire route. At the end of the race, the track log from this receiver can be downloaded to a computer to confirm it was taken to all of the intermediate waypoints without shortcutting. After completing their individual legs, the other contestants can use the exchanged receivers to find their way back to the starting point.

To make it more competitive, different teams shouldn't follow the same route at the same time. If there are only two teams and the geography is uniform, consider having them run the same course in opposite directions. If more than two teams are involved, use staggered starting times.

Organized Activities

You can easily invent variations on the games in this chapter such as combined events involving running, cycling, skiing, and more. Search the web for such topics as "GPS orienteering" to see what events might already be established in your local area. Geocaching is currently the most popular organized GPS activity, but new games regularly pop up on the Internet. For example, Geodashing is a game in which a large number of waypoints throughout the world are posted on the geodashing web page at http://geodashing.gpsgames.org. The object is to reach the most waypoints before the game ends. Waymarking (www.waymarking.com) is a game in which your goal is to find specific types of objects and record their GPS coordinates for others to see. Various other games can be found at http://gpsgames.org.

Trail Mapping with GPS

GPS receivers are ideally suited for creating maps of hiking, biking, and vehicular trails. Simply leave your receiver turned on while you follow the trail, and it will store a complete record of your journey. When you return home, download the data from your GPS receiver into a mapping software program such as National Geographic TOPO! or OziExplorer to plot the trail on a topo map or aerial photograph. This chapter describes how to use your GPS receiver to accurately create custom maps.

Limitations

The first thing to understand is that with a consumer-grade receiver, you won't get the kind of survey-grade accuracy you can achieve with a specialized receiver from a manufacturer such as Trimble or Leica. A survey-grade receiver costs $3,000 to $10,000 and can do several things a consumer unit can't. First, it usually has built-in differential correction (DGPS) capability that can improve accuracy from roughly 10 meters to less than 1 meter (WAAS in a consumer receiver has similar performance, if you can receive the satellite signals). And with access to the appropriate post-processing software, you can be accurate to within a centimeter or two.

Second, a survey-grade unit can automatically record the instantaneous accuracy associated with each track point. When you walk under tree cover and lose satellite lock, a survey-grade receiver flags those data points and allows you to eliminate them from the final record. A consumer receiver, on the other hand, records every track point as if it were just as accurate as every other point—you have to manually identify regions where you lost satellite lock.

Finally, with a survey-grade receiver, the track log can be downloaded as a series of lines and arcs—called a "shapefile"—that are useful in advanced GIS (geographic information system) mapping software programs such as Arcview. A consumer receiver simply records your path as a series of individual dots. (It is possible to convert track logs from Garmin receivers into shapefiles using third-party software.

For more information, refer to the Minnesota Department of Natural Resources web page at www.dnr.state.mn.us/mis/gis/tools/arcview/extensions/DNRGarmin/DNRGarmin.html.)

For trail-mapping purposes, these limitations may not be significant. If you plan to plot the trail on a USGS 7.5-minute topo map, for example, a 7- to 15-meter error is hardly noticeable. It amounts to less than half a millimeter on the final map—about the width of the line used to represent the trail. Shapefiles are important for highway engineers who need very accurate representations of roads, but they are rarely essential for creating recreational trail maps. And if you are attentive while walking the trail, you can manually identify less accurate sections of the track log and adjust them later when creating the final map.

Planning the Hike

Before starting out, you need a plan. If you merely want to walk a trail and record your route, your plan can be simple. But if you want to do things like measure distances between trail junctions, mark the locations of points of interest, or identify areas of the trail that need repair, you need a more detailed plan. Professionals not only record the route of the trail, they also record such information as the trail width, grade, surface type, and the locations of bridges, streams, buildings, signposts, fences, gates, and other points of interest.

This information can be classified into two categories: points and lines (a third category, area, is less important for trail mapping). A signpost, for example, is a point. Its location is recorded as a single waypoint. Trail width is an example of a line. A certain section of the trail may be a single-track footpath, while another section may be a dirt fire road. You would mark the starting and ending points of each section as separate waypoints, together with notes about the trail width along each section.

If you are doing a detailed survey of a trail, you will end up storing lots of waypoints. It is not unusual for a professional to store many hundreds of data points along a 20-kilometer trail. Although you probably won't need that many, it is still wise to use a receiver with the ability to store at least 1,000 waypoints.

Unless you are making a very simple trail map, you will need to take detailed notes as you travel, including each waypoint's name, its distance from the trailhead (as read from the GPS odometer), and specific information about why the waypoint was recorded. You may also want to record repeating information for each waypoint, such as the trail width or surface condition at that waypoint. Some GPS receivers allow you to enter a note with the waypoint, but this process tends to be a

Trail Name:_____ ID:_____

Trail Mapping Record

Date:			Mapped by:	
Waypoint	**Distance**	**Surface**	**Width**	**Notes**

⊠	Trailhead	✖	Trail Junction	🏕 Picnic Area	🚰	Water Source
🌲	Entering Tree Cover	🌲	Campground	🚗 Parking Area	⛏	Point of Interest
🌲	Leaving Tree Cover	🚻	Restroom	)(Bridge	🏛	Sign/Monument

tedious way to record the data and may not allow you to record enough information. You'll probably want a paper log such as the example log sheet shown here.

Many GPS receivers allow you to specify a symbol when marking a waypoint, which can be useful in helping group similar waypoints as you are creating the final map. The Garmin GPSMAP 60Cx, for example, lets you choose from dozens of symbol types in such categories as Outdoors, Points of Interest, Markers, Marine, Civil, Transportation, Navaids, and Signs. You may want to make a list of the different feature types you intend to record, such as trail junctions, bridges, points of interest, signposts, gates, changes in trail width or surface, etc., and the symbol you will use for each feature. The symbol choices in the GPS receiver won't necessarily match up with what you need—you probably won't find a "gate" symbol, for example—but don't worry. Simply pick an existing symbol and use it whenever you reach a gate. Of course, you will need to remember to select the right symbol each time you mark a waypoint, which can become tedious if you record many different types of features.

Finally, you'll need to recognize that if you want to be serious about it, you will need to devote all your attention to mapping the trail. Don't expect to hike it in record time, nor should you expect to do much sightseeing or exploration along the way. Your objective is to travel the trail with no deviations, and you can't afford to be distracted by various detours as you go. If the trail allows, you'll cover distance more quickly on horseback, on a mountain bike, or on an ATV. One advantage of walking, though, is that you will be less tempted to rush past a feature you should have marked as a waypoint.

Think twice about making it a family outing. Spouses and children will quickly get bored stopping every few hundred feet to record a new feature, and you'll soon find it impossible to do an accurate job. If you do bring others along, make sure they are active participants—taking notes, watching for features to be recorded, and helping navigate through regions of poor satellite reception. You will appreciate the extra help.

Recommended Equipment

While most consumer GPS receivers can be used for trail mapping, not every one will work. Here are the things to consider if you are in the market to make a purchase:

Computer interface. A track log doesn't do any good sitting inside a GPS receiver. To be useful, you must transfer it to a computer. This means you must use a receiver that can be connected to one. Although this may seem obvious, be aware that some receivers, most notably the less expensive models in the Magellan eXplorist and Lowrance iFinder lines, don't have this ability. If you expect to do a lot of trail mapping, you may also want to consider a model with a fast USB interface: the PN-40 from DeLorme; the Oregon, GPSMAP 60Cx, eTrex Vista Cx/Legend Cx from Garmin, or the Triton from Magellan, for example.

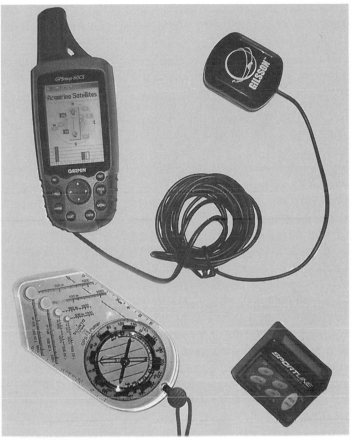

Equipment for creating trail maps (clockwise from top left): GPS receiver, external antenna, pedometer, and magnetic compass

Sensitive receiver. While no receiver is perfect, a more sensitive receiver maintains a better lock on satellites in difficult conditions such as under tree cover or in hilly terrain. Receivers that advertise high-sensitivity receiver technology perform better in difficult conditions.

Large track log memory. The larger the memory, the longer you can go before filling up the track log memory. The Garmin Oregon or GPSMAP 60Cx, each with 10,000 track log points, are good choices, as is the De-Lorme PN-40. The Magellan Triton models have unlimited track point storage via removable SD card.

External antenna. Your GPS receiver must maintain satellite lock the entire time you are navigating the trail. Since satellite signals can't travel through your body, the best solution is to use an external antenna mounted on your head (or hidden discreetly under the crown of a hat). You can then hold the receiver comfortably at your side and monitor the strength of the satellite signals without fear of blocking them. Receivers that can work with an optional external antenna include the Garmin GPSMAP 60Cx, GPSMAP 76Sx, and some models of the Magellan Triton series.

Long battery life and outdoor viewable screen. You'll probably be out on the trail for many hours. You need a rugged receiver designed for extended outdoor use, and one that allows you to replace batteries in the field. You also want a screen display that can be read easily outdoors. These requirements alone almost eliminate PDA or smartphone-based receivers.

For serious work, avoid any receiver that can't be used with an external antenna. Place the antenna inside a hat (Tilley hats have a handy pocket inside the crown you can use for this) and run the cable underneath your clothing to the GPS receiver in your pocket or attached to your belt. Except for the small amount of cable that might be visible running down the back of your neck, it is inconspicuous and keeps your hands free for other things.

You also need a magnetic compass. Aside from helping you keep from getting lost if your GPS receiver fails, it is useful in determining trail bearings in areas of heavy tree cover where the GPS receiver loses satellite lock, a use explained shortly.

Finally, you may want to bring along a separate mechanical pedometer to measure distances along stretches of the trail where a GPS receiver loses satellite lock.

Recording Track Logs in the Field

The following step-by-step instructions describe how to create trail maps suitable for such uses as park maps or hiking guidebooks. Remember, you can't expect to generate survey-grade maps with a consumer GPS receiver.

1.   At the trailhead, take care of all incidental matters (putting on a backpack, saddling horses, visiting the restroom, etc.) before turning on your GPS receiver. Ensure that you have collected everything you need, including notebook, magnetic compass, spare batteries, water bottle, food, first-aid kit, etc.

2.   Ensure that the batteries in your receiver are fresh, and that you are carrying spares. Turn on the receiver and wait for it to enter 3D mode

by locking onto at least four satellites. Confirm the map datum is set correctly (normally WGS 84) and that the coordinate display is set to the desired format (typically either degrees-decimal minutes or UTM).

3. Although not absolutely essential, it is best to delete all existing way-points from the receiver's memory. That way, at the conclusion of the trip, the only waypoints will be the ones you have stored along the way.

4. Only when you are standing at the trailhead and are ready to depart should you mark the trailhead as a GPS waypoint, making sure to select the appropriate waypoint symbol. If your receiver has way-point averaging capability, activate it and remain stationary for at least three minutes before saving the waypoint. If you have deleted all existing waypoints from your receiver's memory, it is fine to just save it with the default waypoint number 001 and go up from there. If you didn't, you will need to give each waypoint a unique name. Record the waypoint information on your log sheet.

5. Once you have marked the trailhead, clear the track log, reset the odometer, confirm that the track log function is turned on, and start the journey. Check the map page to make sure you are recording a track log, but otherwise leave the display set to the satellite page so you can easily monitor satellite signal strengths.

6. Whenever you reach a feature of interest, stop. Mark it as a way-point, remembering to select the appropriate symbol. Use waypoint averaging, if available, and record the details of the feature on your log sheet.

7. Keep the GPS receiver turned on all the time, and don't wander away from the trail. If you must make a detour for some reason, first turn off the receiver. Then return to the exact point of departure before turning it back on. Wait for it to acquire 3D lock before moving.

8. While traveling, keep an eye on the satellite signal strength bars. If you drop out of 3D mode into 2D mode (tracking only three satel-lites), immediately mark the location as a waypoint. Mark another waypoint when you again return to 3D mode. The GPS track log in this region may not be accurate, and you may need to make ad-justments to it on the computer. As you travel this portion of the trail, carefully note how it runs. Is it straight, or does it make sudden turns? Record your observations in the log book. Use your magnetic compass to note the bearing of the trail and how it changes as you move. Use the mechanical pedometer to measure distances along

this portion of the trail. When you transfer the track log into your computer, carefully examine this portion, looking for deviations that don't correlate with your live observations. Manually adjust the GPS track log if necessary.

9. If you completely lose lock and can't even maintain 2D mode, immediately return to the location where you last achieved lock. Mark it as a waypoint and note in your log that this is where you lost lock. One of the disadvantages of a consumer GPS receiver is that when you lose lock, it doesn't immediately tell you. Instead, for about 30 seconds or so, it assumes you are continuing at the same speed and direction as you were when you lost lock. It extrapolates the track log in this direction for a few hundred feet, even if you have stopped (it gets worse the faster you were traveling at the time). If it doesn't reacquire satellites within about 30 seconds, it finally stops recording and tells you that it has lost lock. While this feature may not annoy the casual user, it can play havoc with trail mapping since it results in phantom portions of the track log that have no relation to reality. Again, use your magnetic compass to record the trail bearings and your mechanical pedometer to record the length of each segment in this region. Mark another waypoint when you reacquire lock. After downloading the final track log into your computer, you have to manually delete these inaccurate regions and use your written records to reconstruct this portion of the trail.

10. If your trail is an open-loop route (one in which you return along the same path as you went out), you may want to record the return path as well as the outbound track. If your GPS receiver allows you to save track logs, you might save the outbound track log, then clear it from the active track log and reset the odometer before returning. That way, you have a completely independent record of the return trip. You can later overlay both tracks in the computer to observe how well they align. However, most GPS receivers simplify the track logs when saved; if you want to maintain full resolution, don't clear it from the active track log. There is no need to again record all the previously stored features, though you could discover and mark additional features you missed on the outbound leg.

11. At the end of the trip, save the track log in memory so you don't accidentally overwrite it later (but don't clear it from the active track log). Check over your notes and make necessary clarifications now while they are still fresh in your mind.

Creating a Final Map

Once you have recorded the track log and waypoints, there are several ways to create a final map using commercially available mapping software. The exact details of how to use any specific software program are beyond the scope of this book, so this section focuses on general methods. Let's assume you are using consumer-grade mapping software such as National Geographic's TOPO! State Series or OziExplorer, rather than full-featured—and very expensive—GIS software.

The advantage of a self-contained program like TOPO! is that it includes topographic maps—great if it includes the map for your area of interest, but useless if your trail lies outside the map borders. You can currently obtain TOPO! software for any of the 50 states, as well as certain other areas such as national parks. Its highest-resolution maps are scanned versions of USGS 7.5-minute maps. Unlike paper maps, TOPO! provides seamless coverage of the entire park or state.

National Geographic also sells a version of their software called TOPO! Explorer, a web-based version of TOPO! with a somewhat different user interface. I don't recommend TOPO! Explorer for making custom maps, as it is less flexible and much more difficult to use than the State Series software.

OziExplorer doesn't include maps. You must obtain them separately, either from OziExplorer or from a third-party source. The advantage to this is that with the right map, OziExplorer works for any region in the world. It also works with aerial photographs. Once you have calibrated the map or photo in the program, you can then accurately display track logs and waypoints on it.

Another useful tool for the mapmaker is Google Earth (http://earth.google.com). It is a great supplement to USGS topo maps because it provides up-to-date satellite imagery for the entire world. However, Google Earth isn't a replacement for topo maps. It doesn't show contour lines, it doesn't label features, and in areas of heavy tree cover you won't be able to see such things as roads or trails. Use it to look for changes that have occurred since the date of your topo map. You can often spot differences in road or trail alignments, streams, and even coastlines.

The following process makes use of TOPO! State Series software to create maps suitable for publication. You can use a similar approach with OziExplorer.

Download the waypoints and track log from the GPS receiver into TOPO!. Delete any downloaded waypoints or track logs that are not part of the current project.

Export the TOPO! map to a JPEG using the PRINT MAP function. Select the print boundaries to cover the area of interest without including

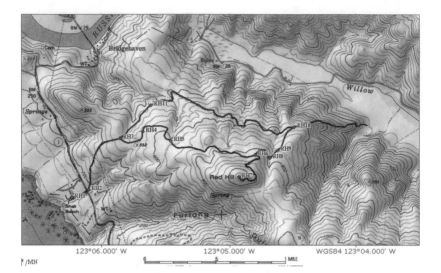

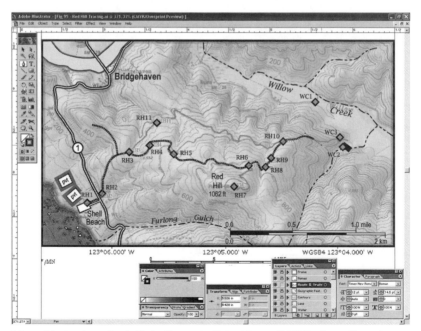

Intermediate steps in creating the final trail map using National Geographic TOPO! software. Above, the tracklog and waypoints have been downloaded to TOPO! and the resulting map exported as a JPEG. In some cases this level of quality may be sufficient. Note the file includes a scale bar at the bottom.

Below, the JPEG file has been imported into Adobe Illustrator and the features are being traced. Note that the water, which will be gray in the final map, and the land, which will be white, have been set to semitransparent so the underlying JPEG file can still be seen. (Map created with TOPO! © 2006 by National Geographic)

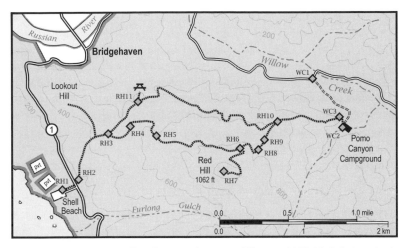

Final map after deleting the JPEG file and resetting the opacity of fill areas to 100%: It includes legend and scale information, index contour lines, and labeled waypoints. The resulting map is clean and easy to read.

more than necessary. If you have many waypoints, you may need to export two versions, one including the waypoints and a less cluttered version showing only the track log. This is where waypoint symbols can be useful. Since you probably won't need to show every type of waypoint on the final map, you can minimize the clutter by exporting only the waypoints with the desired symbols.

For some applications, this JPEG file may be sufficient, although the resulting map has rather low resolution. It is also cluttered with many features, such as contour lines, structures, and shading you may not want in the final map. In this case, you can use a drawing program like Adobe Illustrator to create a simplified map by tracing over only the important features.

Here's how to create a map in Adobe Illustrator. Other graphics programs work similarly:

1. Launch Adobe Illustrator, create a blank page, and import the JPEG file into it. If you know how to use layers, create a specific layer for the JPEG bitmap.

2. Trace over the trail and important features (roads, shorelines, park boundaries, etc.) using the line and polygon drawing tools. Again, if you know how to use layers, create a separate layer on top of the bitmap layer for each type of feature you plan to trace, and keep all the layers locked except for the one you are currently working on. While tracing, set all other layers (except the bitmap layer) to

be invisible. Any filled areas in the current layer should be set to be semi-transparent, at about 20 percent to 50 percent opacity. That way you can still see the underlying JPEG image. Once you have finished tracing, you can set opacity back to 100 percent.

3. If the track log has anomalies from losing satellite lock, adjust the traced line to best represent the actual trail. Refer to your written notes to help reconstruct these portions of the trail.

4. Mark the locations of any exported waypoints you want to appear on the final map.

5. TOPO! includes a map scale at the bottom of the JPEG file. Be sure to include a tracing of this in the final map.

6. Use the text tool to add labels where you want them.

7. It is not usually necessary to copy the contour lines, because they could make the final map look too cluttered. If contour lines are desired, you may want to trace over only the index contours.

8. After you are finished, delete the underlying JPEG file. You will be left with a clean representation of the trail and its relevant surroundings. Refer to the accompanying illustrations on pages 178 and 179 to get a better idea of how to do this.

Highway Navigation with GPS

Before you can explore the outdoors, you have to get there. In the past, that meant fumbling with an oversize paper highway map. Today, you may prefer to use your GPS receiver instead. When loaded with a map of local roads and highways, it can be a useful navigational tool to get you to your starting point, whether it be a distant trailhead or nearby geocache. More expensive receivers can even give turn-by-turn navigation instructions to guide you as you drive.

GPS receivers for highway navigation come in two flavors: those intended expressly for use in a vehicle (including highway navigation software for your smartphone), and those intended primarily for the outdoors. The former have large displays, detailed nationwide road maps, and, most importantly, the ability to provide voice-prompted, turn-by-turn driving instructions. But they don't have the features necessary for outdoor navigation.

The latter are not optimized for use in a vehicle. The displays are much smaller and to use them for highway navigation you must purchase a separate software package from the receiver's manufacturer. They don't typically provide voice guidance; when you approach a turn, they simply beep and display written driving instructions. This makes it unsafe for a driver to navigate alone; it's a two-person job. The driver needs to focus on the road while the navigator reads the GPS display and gives the driving instructions. If you're not willing to do this, don't use your outdoor receiver for highway

The Garmin nüvi 885T is a GPS receiver designed expressly for highway navigation. It can also understand spoken instructions, show current weather conditions, help you avoid traffic backups, check fuel prices, look up movie listings, and check news and stocks. (Courtesy of Garmin)

navigation; the hazard to yourself and others is too great. Instead, buy a separate, in-vehicle system complete with a soothing, synthesized voice to guide you along your way.

With either type of receiver, you need to use commonsense and not blindly trust the displayed instructions. Roads may have changed since the software map was created, or current construction may force you to change plans. And remember that the receiver doesn't know the details of the neighborhoods it directs you through. I once used a handheld, auto-routing GPS receiver as my sole navigation tool on a weeklong business trip throughout the East Coast. It worked flawlessly the entire time until one late night when it directed my colleague and me through the seediest part of a run-down New Jersey suburb, apparently because it was the shortest route to our destination.

Highway Navigation Basics

This chapter assumes you haven't invested in a dedicated highway navigation receiver and want to use your outdoor receiver for guidance. In this case, highway navigation is nothing more than a special version of a multileg route. The "waypoints" for the route are the road intersections where you must make a turn. You navigate from one intersection to the next until you reach your destination.

If you don't have a mapping receiver, you can still do it, but it is a fairly cumbersome process. You must first figure out the route, then manually place a waypoint at the location of each turn. You'll need to place the waypoints using a software program such as Garmin's Map-Source, Magellan's MapSend , or Lowrance's MapCreate. You then create a route and transfer both waypoints and route to your receiver.

If you want to take this simplistic approach, create the waypoints by launching the software program and zooming in on the desired area. Use the program's waypoint tool to place waypoints at the important intersections (you may not want to mark every turn, just the key locations). To keep them straight, name them consecutively, starting from 001.

Once you have placed the waypoints, you are ready to create the route. Open the route page in the computer program and add each waypoint to it in succession. When finished, connect your receiver to the computer and transfer both waypoints and route to it. Once in your receiver, you can activate the route and navigate it just like any other route.

It sounds plausible, but in reality, it's rarely practical for any but the simplest routes. Even driving a fairly short distance may include a dozen or more turns, and it quickly becomes overwhelming to manually create the necessary waypoints. Another problem is that the standard route function in a GPS receiver is designed more for hiking than driving. It doesn't tell you what to do next until you are almost at the waypoint. When driving, that's a problem. Do you turn left or right at the next intersection? Which lane do you need to be in to make the turn? You need to know this long before you get there, and the advantage of a receiver with turn-by-turn guidance is that it prompts you well in advance.

With a non-mapping receiver, the best approach for highway navigation is to create a printed list of driving instructions using a free Internet mapping program such as MapQuest (www.mapquest.com) or Google Maps (http://maps.google.com). In either program, you type in a starting and ending address to get a complete list of driving directions. Alternatively, if you own a software mapping program such as Garmin's City Navigator or DeLorme's Street Atlas USA, you can use it to get a similar list of driving directions. You may want to load your GPS receiver with the latitude-longitude coordinates of a few key intersections (obtained from a suitable mapping program) to help keep you from getting completely lost, but the printed driving directions will serve as your primary navigation tool.

One step up from a non-mapping receiver is a mapping receiver that shows roads and highways but doesn't have the capability for turn-by-turn navigation guidance. The Lowrance iFinder H2Oc and the gray-scale-display Garmin eTrex Vista H are examples of this type of receiver. The iFinder H2Oc can even look up an address for you and show it on the map. Although a definite advantage if your destination is a street

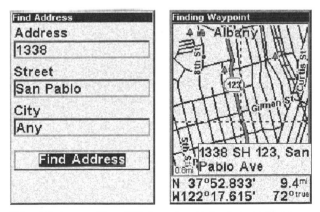

Although the Lowrance iFinder H2Oc does not provide turn-by-turn guidance, it does allow you to look up street addresses and display their locations on the screen.

address or other point of interest, it may not be as helpful if you're heading out to find a geocache.

When the iFinder H2Oc is loaded with detailed street-level maps from MapCreate, you can place waypoints on the map by looking up an address or moving the cursor to the desired location and pushing ENTER. You must then create the route by adding waypoints to it in sequence, as described earlier. Since it can't give turn-by-turn guidance, this type of receiver is best used with printed driving directions. One advantage it affords, though, is that your copilot can watch the GPS receiver's screen to keep you on course and can guide you back if you make a wrong turn.

Turn-by-Turn Guidance

If you expect to do much highway navigation and don't want to invest in a dedicated highway-oriented GPS receiver, you should buy an outdoor receiver that offers turn-by-turn guidance capability. Today, Garmin is the only manufacturer that offers such products. The GPSMAP 60 series and the Oregon series receivers are two good examples. Once loaded with the appropriate software map, either can guide you to a destination along the appropriate roads and highways.

Out of the box, the GPS receiver includes only a high-level base map. To get turn-by-turn guidance, you'll need to install more detailed maps. Not every program is compatible with every receiver, so refer to the Garmin website for specific information. For the GPSMAP 60CSx and Oregon series receivers, Garmin recommends MapSource City Navigator products. Other programs such as Garmin's MapSource MetroGuide will upload similar maps but won't provide turn-by-turn guidance.

Your first task is to get the maps into your receiver. Connect it to your computer's USB port, launch the software program on your computer, and let it detect the GPS receiver. Zoom into the region of interest and click on the map selection tool. Highlight the map regions you want to upload, making sure you don't exceed the receiver's storage limit. (Each time you upload maps, all previous maps are erased, so you always have the full amount of memory available.)

To upload maps using MapSource, select the "transfer" pull-down menu, then "send to device." The time necessary to transfer the files ranges from a few minutes for a single region to several hours if you are uploading the entire U.S. onto a 2 gigabyte memory card. Once the files are stored in your receiver, you won't need your computer again until you want to load a different set of maps.

Navigating to an Address

Once the maps are stored in your receiver, you're ready to navigate. We will use the Garmin GPSMAP 60CSx to illustrate how to navigate to a street address.

After turning on your receiver and letting it acquire its position, push the FIND button. You are given a number of choices, including waypoints, geocaches, cities, points of interest, and addresses. Select ADDRESSES and enter the state, city, number, and street of the desired address. A list of matches appears in the display. Select the correct choice, then choose GOTO. You will be asked if you want to FOLLOW ROAD or go OFF ROAD. Select FOLLOW ROAD (OFF ROAD gives you the direct bearing and distance "as the crow flies"). In a few seconds, your receiver calculates the route and gives you the initial driving instruction. To see a complete list of all driving instructions, push the PAGE button.

It's best to keep the map screen displayed as you drive. As you approach a turn, the receiver beeps and provides written instructions for what to do. Have your copilot read the instructions so you can stay focused on driving. Continue following the instructions until you reach your destination.

You can also navigate to any stored waypoint. Simply call up the waypoint using the FIND button, select GOTO, and specify FOLLOW ROAD. Note that if the waypoint is not along a road, the software guesses as to where you

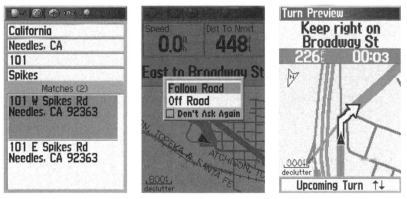

The simplified sequence for navigating to a street address using the GPSMAP 60CSx: After pushing the FIND button, choose ADDRESSES (upper left). Enter the address and select the desired choice from the list of matches. After selecting GOTO, choose the FOLLOW ROAD option. The receiver automatically calculates the route and guides you to your destination using text messages displayed on screen (right).

should exit the road. Use commonsense and good judgment when deciding whether this is an appropriate exit.

When using FOLLOW ROAD with the GPS MAP 60CSx, you can select from several routing options. Route choices include fastest time or shortest distance, and you can customize the route depending on whether you are driving a car, bicycle, or truck. You can also choose to avoid certain types of roads. Remember, though, that you still need to exercise commonsense to avoid unexpected problems as you navigate.

Other Recommendations

Besides using a copilot, keep a few other practicalities in mind. Your receiver may not pick up satellite signals very well when it's inside an automobile. It will do better when placed on the dashboard where it can "see" through the windshield, rather than inside under the car's metal roof. Don't just lay it on the dashboard though; you'll need to secure it to prevent it from sliding around and becoming a dangerous projectile as you turn. If your receiver can accept an external antenna, consider investing in one. Put the antenna where it has a good view of the sky, and keep the GPS receiver conveniently nearby. Although I've seen some people recommend that the external antenna

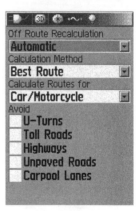

You can select from several navigation options when using the FOLLOW ROAD option on the GPSMAP 60CSx.

be magnetically mounted to the outside roof of the car, I've had excellent success attaching it to the rearview mirror by wrapping the cable several times snugly around the mirror support post. Newer GPS units with high-sensitivity receiver chips don't need an external antenna.

If you can't get your receiver to work anywhere inside your car, it may be because your automobile windshield has a metallic coating that interferes with satellite signal reception. If so, you'll have to use an external antenna attached to the outside roof, with the antenna cable routed through a slightly open window.

Finally, consider investing in an external power cord designed to run your receiver from your car's 12-volt power outlet. You don't want to run your batteries down before you even get to the starting point.

15

GPS Receiver Selection Guide

T his chapter briefly reviews various GPS receivers suitable for outdoor recreational use. Equipment manufacturers constantly update their product lines; before making a purchase decision, visit your local outdoor specialty shop or do research on the Internet to get current information. A good starting point is http://gpsinformation. net, which covers a wide range of GPS-related subjects. You might also want to watch or join the discussions on the Google GPS newsgroup site at http://groups.google.com/group/sci.geo.satellite-nav/topics.

The receivers described here were expressly designed for use in the outdoors, and the emphasis is on products for the North American market. This chapter doesn't cover such specialty products as receivers designed to work through a mobile phone or PDA, GPS wristwatches, or products intended primarily for marine, aircraft, or automobile use. I strongly believe that if you intend to use GPS in the outdoors, you need a receiver specifically designed for that purpose. While it might be reasonable to use a mobile phone–based GPS receiver for geocaching in a neighborhood park, it's a poor tradeoff in the wilderness. You'll make large sacrifices in the unit's ruggedness, water resistance, battery life, and ease of use. As both mobile phones and their GPS capabilities continue to improve, this situation might someday change.

The receivers described here all have at least 12 parallel channels and meet the minimum requirements laid out in Chapter 2. Most will do much more. At a minimum, they can:

▶ Report your position in latitude and longitude or UTM

▶ Select from different map datums, including WGS 84 and NAD 27

▶ Determine your speed and direction of travel

▶ Store at least 500 waypoint locations

▶ Calculate the direction and distance from your current location to any stored waypoint, and from one waypoint to another

▶ Plot track logs of your journeys

▶ Withstand at least 30 minutes of immersion in 1 meter of water, per the IEC 529 IPX7 standard

Garmin International, Inc.

Garmin (www.garmin.com) is a long-established manufacturer of GPS equipment that offers several product families for the outdoor recreation market, from the diminutive Geko to the full-size GPSMAP 76CSx. You'll find a Garmin receiver for just about every combination of feature set and price point.

Oregon Family

The Oregon family is Garmin's current top-of-the-line product family for the outdoor navigator. All Oregon models include large, high-resolution 1.5 x 2.5-inch color touch screen displays (200 x 450 pixels). Each includes a high-sensitivity receiver, built-in magnetic compass and barometric altimeter, and the ability to add additional maps. All models can perform turn-by-turn highway navigation when loaded with a compatible map from Garmin's MapSource product family.

The least expensive model is the Oregon 300, which comes loaded only with a high-level base map. Next up is the Oregon 400, which has three versions. All include the high-level base map; the 400c adds preloaded coastal charts for mariners, while the 400i adds preloaded maps of inland waterways. The 400t, designed for land navigators, adds de-

Garmin Oregon and Dakota receivers

tailed topographic maps (1:100,000 scale). The Oregon 450, introduced in early 2010, is designed to eventually replace the model 300. It incorporates a new 3-axis magnetic compass that accurately measures compass directions in any orientation (the 300's 2-axis compass must be held level to make an accurate reading). The Oregon 450t is intended to replace the model 400t and also incorporates the 3-axis compass.

The two high-end Oregon models are the 550 and 550t. Both have the 3-axis compass and both include a 3.2 megapixel camera. The 550 comes factory-loaded with only the high-level base map, while the 550t adds the 1:100,000 topo map. Both models automatically geotag their photos.

The Oregon family of products is especially targeted at geocachers. All models work seamlessly with the http://geocaching.com website, allowing you to store locations, terrain, difficulty, hints, and descriptions. They also support wireless sharing of waypoints, routes, tracks, and geocaches with other Oregon, Dakota, and Colorado receivers.

The Oregon's user interface has been designed to take maximum advantage of the touch screen display. Rather than having to scroll sequentially through a list of pages, you simply touch the icon for the desired page from the main screen. Conceptually, it is similar to the icon-based design of smartphones such as the Apple iPhone, although the implementation is somewhat different.

To conserve battery life the Oregon uses a transreflective TFT display that doesn't require backlighting in well-lit environments. The main tradeoff with this approach is a screen that is fairly dim even in bright light. Garmin has simplified the user interface compared to previous products like the GPSMAP 60CSx. In most cases this change isn't a problem, but you may discover some favorite features from the 60CSx are missing from the Oregon. For example, the route listing in the Oregon only shows the waypoint names; it doesn't show the bearing and distance between successive waypoints.

Dakota Family

The two products in this family are essentially smaller versions of the Oregon. They have 1.4 x 2.2-inch color touch screen displays (160 x 240 pixels), high-sensitivity receivers, built-in base maps, and 850 MB of internal memory for loading additional maps. With a compatible MapSource map installed, either can do turn-by-turn highway navigation. Both include a geocaching mode similar to the Oregon.

The simpler of the two, the Dakota 20 lacks a magnetic compass or barometric altimeter and doesn't accept external memory cards. The Dakota 20 adds an altimeter and 3-axis compass and can accept microSD cards. The Dakota user interface is similar to the Oregon, and Dakota units can wirelessly share data with other Dakota or Oregon receivers. This compatibility makes the Dakota attractive as a back-up unit to the Oregon for explorers who venture far from civilization.

Colorado Family

These products are somewhat similar to the Oregon but lack the touch screen display. Instead, you make your selections using a combination wheel and four-way rocker switch (called a "Rock 'n Roller®" by Garmin) located above the display. All four family members include a 1.5 x 2.6-inch high resolution display (240 x 400 pixels), a high-sensitivity receiver, barometric altimeter, and 2-axis electronic compass. All accept optional SD cards and can provide turn-by-turn navigation when loaded with optional highway maps. The software features of the Colorado are not identical to the Oregon, so if certain lesser-used features are important to you, it would be wise to verify they are included before you buy.

The Colorado 300 is the least expensive model. It comes loaded only with a high-level base map. The Colorado 400c includes BlueChart coastal maps and is designed for mariners. The Colorado 400i includes a detailed map of inland lakes and waterways, while the Colorado 400t includes detailed topographic maps (1:100,000 scale).

GPSMAP 60 Family

Although Garmin has introduced several newer product lines, many people still consider the GPSMAP 60 family to be the gold standard for outdoor receivers because of its rugged construction, bright display, and extensive list of software features. The newest products, the GPS-MAP 62, 62s, and 62st, introduced in mid-2010, bring the best features of the Oregon and Dakota line to this family. The GPSMAP 62 is a mapping receiver with auto-routing capability that includes a color display easily viewed in sunlight, a built-in basemap, 1.7 GB memory, and compatibility with Garmin Custom Maps and most MapSource products. The GPSMAP 62s adds a 3-axis compass, barometric altimeter, and microSD memory slot. The GPSMAP 62st further adds 1:100,000-scale U.S. topo maps. Although they don't have touch screens, their user interface is similar to the Oregon and Dakota. All three products support paperless geocaching.

The GPSMAP 60Cx and 60CSx are also mapping receivers with an older user interface that doesn't support paperless geocaching or Garmin Custom Maps. The compass in the 60CSx is a less versatile 2-axis design that must be held level to obtain an accurate reading. The less expensive GPSMAP 60 uses a four-level grayscale display, and the low-cost GPS 60 is a non-mapping receiver with 1 megabyte of memory that can be used to store cities and other points of interest.

The well-designed keypads on these receivers include MARK and FIND buttons, as well as a multipurpose, four-direction rocker switch. It is used to enter waypoint coordinates and names, select from various menu choices, and pan the map display horizontally and vertically.

All GPSMAP 60 receivers use a sensitive quadrifilar helix antenna. Battery life is claimed to be as much as 20 hours for products with color displays and 28 hours for those with grayscale displays. All include Garmin's proprietary USB interface for high-speed data transfer.

GPSMAP 60CSx (Garmin International)

eTrex Family

Really two separate families with the same name, the eTrex "classic" receivers described here have grayscale displays. The eTrex HC products, described in the next section, have color displays and a different user interface in a slightly wider package.

The three products in the classic eTrex family range from the basic yellow eTrex H with its bare-minimum feature set to the full-featured Vista H. The two more expensive members of the family incorporate a thumb-operated joystick (formerly called the "thumb stick") that provides a better user interface than the simple push buttons of the basic eTrex H.

The plain, yellow eTrex H is the least expensive member of the family. It doesn't have internal maps and doesn't include any additional features like magnetic compasses or barometric altimeters. Today's

eTrex Venture (Garmin International)

eTrex H is an improved version of a product originally introduced in 1999. The "H" indicates it has a high-sensitivity receiver with WAAS capability. It can store 500 waypoints, 20 routes, and up to 10 saved tracks. If you don't mind using paper maps and don't want to spend a lot of money, the basic eTrex H is a reasonable choice, but bear in mind you won't be able to upgrade it if you later want more features.

Next lowest in price, the Legend H is the least expensive eTrex mapping receiver. Its 24 MB of internal memory is sufficient to store street maps of a small state or topo maps of a large national park. It comes with a built-in base map and is compatible with all MapSource products, although it can't perform turn-by-turn navigation.

The top end of the classic eTrex line is the Vista H, also with 24 MB of internal memory. It includes a separate electronic compass and a barometric altimeter, and like the Legend H, it can store 1,000 waypoints, 20 routes, and 10 tracks. It, too, is WAAS compatible.

All eTrex products are small, lightweight, and fairly rugged. The user interface is spartan, with a minimum number of dedicated keys limited to PAGE, ENTER, POWER, and an UP/DOWN rocker switch. The Legend H and Vista H include the thumb stick and are a little easier to use.

All eTrex receivers use a rectangular patch antenna (visible through the translucent case of the Legend H) that isn't quite as sensitive under heavy tree cover as that of larger receivers such as the GPSMAP 60Cx. Since the internal memory in these receivers is not accessible by users, it isn't possible to increase it or swap memory cards. The Legend H and Vista H connect to a computer through a USB port, allowing you to transfer waypoints, routes, and tracks in either direction, and to upload MapSource maps to the receiver. The basic eTrex H still uses the old RS-232 serial port interface.

eTrex HCx Family

Although superficially similar to the eTrex classic family, these four receivers have color displays and are more like baby versions of the GPSMAP 60 family. The Venture HC has a color display, 24 MB of internal memory, and a built-in base map. The next step up is the Summit HC, which adds a barometric altimeter and magnetic compass. The Legend HCx doesn't have internal memory. Instead, it accepts an optional microSD memory card, and with

eTrex Vista HCx (Garmin International)

optional City Navigator software it can provide turn-by-turn guidance to any address you specify (text guidance only, no voice command capability). The top-of-the-line Vista HCx adds a barometric altimeter and magnetic compass. All "H" models use a high-sensitivity receiver, and all connect to a computer via Garmin's proprietary USB interface. Battery life ranges between 14 and 25 hours depending on the model.

GPSMAP 76 Family

The products in this family are especially popular for marine applications, but are very suitable for general outdoor use. These units are physically larger than the GPSMAP 60 series, but with a similar size display. They have eight dedicated keys and a four-position rocker switch used to make menu selections. All three models are WAAS compatible. They all use quadrifilar helix antennas and include an external antenna connector.

The basic GPSMAP 76 has 8 MB of memory and 10 track logs. It is compatible with all MapSource products. The GPSMAP 76Cx includes a high-sensitivity receiver, a 256-color, daylight-readable display, and 128 MB of removable microSD memory.

GPSMAP 76CSx (Garmin International)

The GPSMAP 76CSx adds a barometric altimeter and a magnetic compass.

Products in the GPSMAP 76 family are a good choice for people who want to do a lot of highway or marine navigation in addition to wilderness exploration. The tradeoff is greater size and weight when you're out on a hike. Note that the GPSMAP 60Cx and 60CSx have the same size display and are otherwise similar in a slightly smaller package.

Geko Family

The two members of this family are remarkably small and light. They measure in at a little less than 4 inches high, 2 inches wide, and 1 inch thick. At only 2.3 ounces,

Geko 201 (Garmin International)

they are less than half the weight of an eTrex. The Geko 201 can store 500 waypoints, 20 routes, and 10,000 track log points. It meets what I consider the minimum requirements for general outdoor use. The Geko 301 adds a barometric altimeter and magnetic fluxgate compass. Since neither is a mapping receiver, they are impractical for in-vehicle use. They connect to a computer using the old RS-232 serial port. To achieve their small size, they employ two AAA batteries, giving them nine to 12 hours of useful life per set. Gekos do not have high-sensitivity receivers.

Rino Family

The Rino, an acronym for "Radio Integrated with Navigation for the Outdoors," is a GPS receiver integrated with a two-way radio. There are currently five models: the Rino 110, 120, 130, 520HCx, and 530HCx.

The two-way radio capability in these receivers is unique. Rinos can broadcast on both the free Family Radio Service (FRS) channels and the more powerful General Mobile Radio System (GMRS) frequencies, which require an $85 FCC license. The license is assigned to a specific adult, not a specific radio, and the FCC permits immediate family members of the licensee to use more than one radio to communicate with each other under one license. Nonfamily members would need separate licenses. (Regulations sometimes change, so make sure you understand current law before using GMRS frequencies.) If you intend to use GMRS frequencies, don't forget to purchase this license—unlicensed use can result in a fine of $10,000 per day. For more information, visit the FCC website at http://wireless.fcc.gov/services/index.htm?job=service_home&id=general_mobile.

The GPS portion of the Rino 110 has 1 megabyte internal memory that can be used to store only points of interest, not complete maps. The Rino 120 increases the internal memory to 8 MB and adds full MapSource compatibility. The Rino 130 has 24 MB of memory, plus a built-in barometric

Rino 530HCx (Garmin International)

altimeter, magnetic compass, and NOAA weather radio. All models in the 100 series have grayscale displays.

The 500-series Rinos are distinguished by their color displays and more modern GPS capabilities. The Rino 520 has no internal memory but accepts optional microSD memory cards. It includes a USB interface, turn-by-turn auto routing capability, and a more powerful GMRS two-way radio. The Rino 530 adds the barometric altimeter and magnetic compass. Both models in the 500 series have high-sensitivity GPS receivers, but neither includes an NOAA weather radio.

Canadian law has recently changed and now permits two-way radio transmission on GMRS frequencies, although older Rinos sold in Canada don't include this capability. Unlike the U.S., Canada does not charge a license fee for use of GMRS frequencies. Outside of Canada and the U.S., check local laws before using any FRS or GMRS radio, as many countries prohibit their use.

The two-way radio can communicate with any FRS or GMRS radio. If you already own one, you don't have to buy more than one Rino. If you do, though, you get certain advantages: Two Rinos can transmit and display their positions on each others' map screens, letting you track the location and movement of the other person. In the past, the FCC permitted this use only on FRS frequencies, but recent rule changes now allow it on GMRS frequencies. Owners of older Rinos can download a free software update to add this capability.

Lowrance Electronics, Inc.

Lowrance (www.lowrance.com) is well-known for their line of sport fishing SONAR fish finders and their marine and aircraft navigation equipment. The company is also an established player in the recreational outdoor market through its iFinder line of GPS receivers.

Endura Family

Lowrance introduced their newest product family, the Endura, in mid-2009. All three models have 42-channel GPS receivers that include WAAS reception. All have 2.7-inch (diagonal) 320 x 240-pixel color touch screen displays together with physical buttons that replicate the main touch screen functionalities. In normal use, all selections can be made using the touch screen. The physical buttons are said to be easier to use when wearing gloves in cold weather.

The Endura Out&Back is the least expensive model. It can store 2,000 waypoints, 60 routes, and 3,000 geocaches. It includes a high-level base map plus a microSD card slot that accepts up to 32 GB of memory for more detailed maps. Next up is the Endura Safari, which adds a barometric altimeter and 3-axis electronic compass, plus the ability to do turn-by-turn highway navigation when loaded with optional maps. At the high end is the Endura Safari, which adds another 4 GB internal memory, high-resolution topographic maps, and NAVTEQ® road maps for the continuous 48 states.

iFinder Family

The five models in this line can be divided into two families: those with grayscale displays and those with color displays. All iFinders currently sold are waterproof to the IPX7 standard, although older units are not. All have built-in base maps and all except the GO2 have external antenna connectors.

The basic iFinder GO2 has a 16-channel receiver, a 2-inch grayscale display, and 64 MB of internal memory preloaded with a U.S. base map that includes marine navigation aids. It can store 1,000 waypoints and 100 tracks (called "trails" by Lowrance). Each trail can hold up to 10,000 points.

The iFinder H2O, iFinder Hunt, and iFinder Explorer are 12-channel receivers with 3-inch grayscale displays. They have built-in U.S. base maps and slots for optional MMC or SD memory cards to hold more detailed maps. The iFinder Explorer includes a built-in barometric altimeter and a magnetic compass. The iFinder Hunt is basically an Explorer with a customized hunting mode of operation. It also includes a unique voice-recording capability that allows you to attach audible notes to waypoints. All are compatible with Lowrance MapCreate software, as well as their various marine- and lake-mapping software products.

The iFinder H2OC, Hunt C, and Expedition C are 16-channel receivers with color displays. Like their grayscale counterparts, they include built-in U.S. base maps and slots for optional MMC or SD memory cards. They work with Lowrance MapCreate software. The Expedition C includes a barometric altimeter, magnetic compass, and the voice recording capability. It can also play MP3 audio files stored on the MMC card. The Hunt C is like an Expedition C with a slightly smaller screen and the customized hunting mode of operation.

iFinder H2OC (Courtesy of Lowrance)

All Lowrance iFinder products have an RS-232 serial port conforming to the NMEA 0183 data transfer standard, the dominant standard for the boating industry, which is a strong market for Lowrance. Be aware that the serial port on some iFinders is not designed to interface to a computer, but rather to marine equipment such as autopilots. For units with removable memory, this isn't really a problem because the memory card connects to a computer through a separate SD/MMC high-speed USB card reader.

DeLorme

DeLorme (www.delorme.com) is a major manufacturer of paper and software topographic and highway maps. Their flagship products are Street Atlas USA and TopoUSA, two well-regarded software programs. Street Atlas USA is a vector graphics map with street-level detail of the U.S. and Canada. TopoUSA is a vector graphics topo map of the entire U.S. with resolution similar to USGS 7.5-minute topo maps.

Earthmate GPS PN Family

DeLorme offers several receivers for outdoor navigators. The low-end PN-20, introduced in 2007, is being phased out in favor of the improved PN-30. The PN-30 uses a true 32-channel, WAAS-enabled chipset from STMicroelectronics to deliver fast acquisition time under almost all conditions. It includes 500 MB of internal memory, support for SD and SDHC memory cards, a fast USB interface connection, a paperless geocaching mode, a user-friendly keypad with dedicated MARK and FIND buttons, and a four-way rocker switch. It can store up to 1,000 waypoints and 10 tracks of up to 10,000 points each. The PN-40 adds a true barometric altimeter and 3-axis magnetic compass.

In early 2010, DeLorme introduced the newest members of the family, the PN-60 and PN-60w. Building on the PN-40, these two models include 3.5 GB of internal memory, an ambient light sensor that controls screen backlight level, and the barometric altimeter and 3-axis magnetic compass. The PN-60w is especially interesting. DeLorme has partnered with SPOT, a satellite messaging company, to give you the ability to

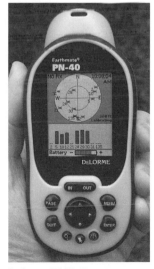

Earthmate GPS PN-40

send text messages that include your position even when you are outside the range of a cellular network. If you regularly travel off the beaten path, you may find this useful for sending "All OK" or "SOS" messages to family back home. This optional service is available for an additional monthly fee. The PN-60w also includes a wireless feature that lets you send your position to other nearby PN-60w users up to about half a mile away.

The Earthmate PN-family receivers offer several unique and interesting capabilities. They are compatible with TopoUSA, which is included with the purchase of the receiver. Besides allowing you to transfer waypoints and tracks, you can also transfer TopoUSA topo maps into the receiver. In addition, the PN-family receivers were the first outdoor-oriented receivers to allow you to load aerial photographs and scanned versions of USGS 7.5-minute topo maps for display on the receiver's screen. The aerial photos and USGS topo maps must be purchased from DeLorme by downloading from their website (a limited number of downloads are included free with the receiver). Once you have loaded the photos and maps, you can quickly switch between the various topographic and photographic views for any location of interest.

DeLorme receivers don't use a GOTO command. Instead, you always use the ROUTE command, even for a direct GOTO function. Once you get used to this approach it isn't a problem, and PN-series receivers perform similarly to other GPS receivers.

Magellan Navigation, Inc.

Magellan (www.magellangps.com) offers a range of consumer GPS receivers for highway and outdoor navigation. Its main products for the outdoor market are the Triton family of receivers.

Triton Family

Magellan's Triton family offers several unique benefits. They are the first outdoor receivers to accept maps from National Geographic's TOPO! and Weekend Explorer mapping software. They can display true USGS 7.5-minute topo maps similar to the Delorme PN-40, but with the added ability to display all five scales of National Geographic maps. Like the PN-40, multiple maps can be layered on a single device, allowing you to load Magellan's topographic maps or marine cartography and National Geographic maps at the same time. All members of the family are waterproof to the IPX7 standard, and the high-end members include a color touch-screen display.

The Triton 200 is the least expensive family member. This basic unit includes a 2.2-inch QVGA color display, a built-in base map, plus a number of preprogrammed points of interest. The Triton 300 includes 10 MB of internal memory for storing additional maps, while the Triton 400 adds an SD card slot for unlimited removable memory. The Triton 500 adds a 3-axis electronic compass and barometric altimeter.

The two high-end members of the family are the Triton 1500 and Triton 2000. Both have a larger 2.7-inch QVGA color touch screen, SD card slot, built-in audio voice recorder, and LED flashlight. The Triton 2000 includes a 2 megapixel digital camera, 3-axis electronic compass, and barometric altimeter.

Triton 2000

GPS Accessories

There are only a few GPS accessories I consider essential. Most important, in my opinion, is a sturdy case. GPS receivers are delicate pieces of electronic equipment, so when you are out in the wilderness, they need as much protection as possible. You can use generic cases designed for compact digital cameras or a custom case specifically designed by the manufacturer for your receiver.

If you own a mapping receiver, you'll probably want to invest in the appropriate software mapping program from your receiver's manufacturer. That way, you can load more detailed maps than are available from the built-in base map, limited only by the amount of receiver memory.

Both Garmin (MapSource) and Magellan (MapSend) offer several alternatives, depending on your needs. You can choose from topographic, highway, or marine maps. With the right receiver, a highway map can guide you to an exact street address. Topo maps are great for the outdoor adventurer but can't automatically guide you to a destination. Since they are based on USGS topo maps, their road detail is not as current as a true highway-mapping program. If you buy a topo program, make sure you know the level of detail you are getting. Some programs provide the equivalent of 1:100,000 paper maps, while a few offer detail similar to a 1:24,000 USGS 7.5-minute map.

DeLorme's PN-series receivers are compatible with TopoUSA software. They also offer the unique ability to download aerial photographs and scanned copies of USGS topo maps from the DeLorme website. When all three are loaded into the receiver, you can quickly switch among different displays.

Lowrance uses the MapCreate software, which combines highway, topographic, and marine databases. It is also available pre-loaded on MMC cards—particularly convenient for extended trips where you can't easily upload new maps from a computer to your receiver as you travel.

To connect your receiver to a personal computer, you'll need the appropriate interface cable. Newer receivers use standard USB cables, but older receivers use RS-232 serial cables. Since these are custom designs, your best bet is to purchase the cable offered by your receiver's manufacturer. You can sometimes save money by purchasing a third-party cable off the Internet, but the quality of such products varies widely.

Another useful cable is one that lets you connect your receiver to an automobile cigarette lighter socket. If you intend to use your receiver in a vehicle, you won't want to depend on battery power. Again, this is a custom-designed cable best purchased from the manufacturer of your receiver. You may also need to use this cable if you want to run your receiver from a 110-volt outlet. Most receivers don't offer a convenient way to plug into AC power, so you may need to purchase an adapter that converts 110 volts AC to 12 volts DC through a cigarette lighter socket. Then plug your automobile adapter into this socket.

Finally, an Internet search on the words "GPS accessories" will yield an almost unlimited range of products of varying usefulness. Depending on your intended use, you might invest in such accessories as a bicycle handlebar mount, external antenna, PDA interface cable, automobile mount, training video, rechargeable batteries, or a wide variety of other software products.

Appendix I

GPS FAQs

These days, lists of frequently asked questions, or FAQs, are all the rage. It seems incomplete to offer a book on GPS navigation that doesn't include some sort of FAQ list, so here it is. Many of these topics have already been covered elsewhere in the book, but they are conveniently collected here in one place for easy reference. Some of the topics, ones of general interest but not essential for outdoor navigators, are covered here for the first time.

My GPS instruction manual makes it sound like I only need to track three satellites to find my position. You say I need four. What's the story?

To *accurately* find your position, you need to be tracking four satellites. Many GPS instruction manuals don't explain very well. They might say something like, "With three satellites, your receiver does not report elevation." This explanation makes it sound like your horizontal position is still reported accurately, but this is not necessarily the case. To get good results, your receiver needs accurate elevation information. The fourth satellite gives it the ability to make that calculation. Without a fourth satellite, it must assume an elevation. The only one it knows is the last one it measured, but if you've changed position since then, your current elevation could be considerably different. The result could be an error of a mile or more from your true position. When it is critical that you know your exact position, don't believe your GPS receiver unless it is tracking at least four satellites.

Is my GPS receiver's readout of speed very accurate?

Yes, it is quite accurate, even better than the speedometer in your car. Contrary to what many people think, your receiver does not measure speed by calculating how fast your position changes. If it did, it would be much less accurate. It calculates speed by measuring the Doppler shifts of the satellite signals—the same principle that police radar guns use to determine how fast a car is traveling, with a similar accuracy.

How accurately can my GPS receiver find my position?

Unfortunately, that's not an easy question to answer. It depends on several factors, some in your control, others not. The number of satellites being tracked and their locations in the sky are very important. Ideally, you want to be tracking one satellite overhead and three more spaced equally around you midway up from the horizon. Four satellites in a straight line is the worst configuration. Other error sources include atmospheric effects and the current level of solar activity (such things as sunspots and solar flares).

It's safe to assume that when locked on to at least four satellites, your GPS receiver can find its position to within about 50 feet. Most of the time, it will be much better, approaching 25 feet or less. On rare occasions, it may be worse. It is not possible to reliably achieve accuracies in the range of 10 feet or less without WAAS or DGPS. And yes, the more satellites you are tracking, the better the accuracy.

Does GPS work underwater?

No. Even an inch of water is enough to completely block the satellite signals and prevent your receiver from finding its position. Receivers are designed to be waterproof so that they won't get damaged if you use them in the rain or if they accidentally get dunked in a lake or river. They cannot find your position underwater.

What about rain and clouds? Don't they also block the satellite signals?

No, water vapor or isolated droplets don't have much of an effect on the satellite signals (for the engineers in the crowd, the attenuation is less than 2 dB). The only thing you might have to worry about is if your receiver's antenna gets coated with water as a result of heavy rain. But in that case, you can simply wipe the water away and solve the problem.

Why does my receiver lose satellite lock under heavy tree cover?

Tree leaves are full of water. It's like having a solid film of water between you and the satellites. Depending on its design, a receiver may be more or less sensitive to this effect. A receiver with a good, high-gain antenna and low-noise electronics will do somewhat better than a receiver with a smaller antenna and less expensive circuitry. But no receiver will work well under heavy tree cover.

How accurate is my receiver as an altimeter?

The GPS readout of altitude is not very accurate, despite what you may read in Internet chat groups. Several factors come into play: First, the

GPS system wasn't designed to measure altitude (called "elevation" in GPS language) accurately. The problem comes in the design of the satellite orbits. The details are fairly technical, but simply stated, the orbits are well-designed for measuring horizontal positions, not for vertical positions. The vertical measurement uncertainty is about three times worse than horizontal uncertainty.

Another problem comes from how elevation is defined: Topo maps and elevation signs report altitude referenced to mean sea level. Your GPS receiver measures it against a mathematical model of the earth. This model can be tens of feet different from true mean sea level in some areas. Overall, you can't expect a GPS receiver to measure elevation to better than a few hundred feet accuracy, and in some cases it can be much worse. If you want to accurately measure elevation, you must use a calibrated barometric altimeter. Some more expensive receivers include a separate barometric altimeter just for this purpose.

How good is my GPS receiver as a compass?

That's a trick question. A GPS receiver doesn't really function as a true compass. Its "compass" page shows what direction you are *moving*, not what direction it is *pointed*. If you stop moving, it stops working. It is actually a heading indicator, not a compass. When you are moving faster than about 10 miles per hour, it does a very good job. Below that speed, electrical noise and system inaccuracies introduce more errors. It is still pretty good, though. I've never had a problem using the compass page to guide me to a hidden geocache, as long as I have kept moving.

Some GPS receivers have a separate, built-in electronic compass. This is a true magnetic compass separate from the GPS functionality. These types of compasses can find a bearing to an accuracy of 5 degrees or less, similar to an ordinary baseplate compass. It's an expensive addition to your receiver and eats up batteries rapidly, so you should still carry a separate baseplate compass.

How accurate is the GPS receiver in my iPhone, Blackberry, or Android smartphone?

The first generation of smartphones did not include true GPS receivers; they calculated their position using the signals from the cell phone towers, which was not very accurate. Newer smartphones include GPS receivers, but they still don't replace a dedicated GPS receiver. Smartphone designers make tradeoffs to improve performance in populated areas at the expense of performance in the wilderness. To reduce the time it takes to find your position, a smartphone obtains almanac and ephemeris data from the cell phone network rather than from the satellites. This method works well as long as it is within range of a cell phone tower, but if it isn't, your smartphone might not be able to find its position. Another problem is that a smartphone is not as rugged as a dedicated GPS receiver. For example, a handheld GPS receiver is designed to be waterproof, but a smartphone isn't; getting it wet will usually void its warranty. Finally, using your smartphone's GPS capability quickly depletes its batteries. With its GPS function turned on continuously, you may only get 2 to 3 hours of battery life.

Will my GPS receiver work inside a commercial aircraft?

It's possible. You need to be sitting at a window seat with your receiver pressed right up against the window. If you're lucky, the satellites will be in exactly the right positions, and you can lock onto at least a few. (Even 2D mode is useful here since a mile or two error in location will still give you a good idea of where you are.)

It may take a lot longer for your receiver to get a position fix because you are traveling in the neighborhood of 600 miles per hour. (You'll see your exact speed when your receiver is locked on.)

A more important question is whether you are even allowed to operate a GPS receiver inside an aircraft. As of this writing, there are no laws prohibiting the use of GPS receivers in the U.S.; it is strictly up to the individual airlines. Some airlines allow you to operate a receiver after the aircraft has reached cruising altitude, while others prohibit it at all times. None allows you to operate it during the critical takeoff and landing phases. Check http://gpsinformation.net for a current listing of various airline policies.

Does my GPS receiver send out a signal the government or anyone else can use to track my location?

No. GPS is a completely passive system. You can receive signals from the satellites, but your receiver is not a transmitter. It doesn't broadcast any kind of information about your position. Like almost all electronics, though, it does emit very low levels of radio waves that could theoretically interfere with the operation of sensitive equipment nearby. That is why airlines won't let you use a GPS receiver (or any other electronic device) during takeoff or landing.

How is a route different from a track?

A route is something you create and enter into your receiver. It is a collection of waypoints you have organized into a specific sequence. When navigating a route, your receiver guides you from one waypoint to the next in sequence. When you arrive at one waypoint, it automatically switches to guide you to the next one. Your receiver can only show you the straight-line path from one waypoint to the next.

A track (called a "trail" by some manufacturers) is not something you manually enter. It is a detailed record of the exact path you have been following. When you activate the tracking function, your GPS receiver automatically plots track points at regular intervals to map your path. There may be hundreds or thousands of points on a track, but they are not named waypoints. And you can't easily read latitudes and longitudes of track points like you can for waypoints.

What is the "track back" function?

Many receivers offer a way to easily reverse your outbound track and follow it back to its origin. In this mode, your receiver automatically creates a route from its stored track. This feature can be useful if you need to closely follow your exact path back to where you started. This "track back" route creates a series of phantom waypoints along your original track that lets you return the same way you came. Since a "track back" route consists of only a limited number of waypoints, it does not include all the detail of the original track.

Why does my receiver sometimes report fantastic speeds of many hundreds of miles per hour or show large, rapid variations in my position, even when I am standing still?

This error is the result of a problem called multipath error. You'll usually see it in difficult terrain like canyons, mountainous regions, or heavy tree cover, and in cities with numerous tall buildings. Your GPS receiver determines its position by measuring the time it takes a radio signal to travel from a satellite to the receiver assuming the signal traveled in a straight line. Objects like mountains or skyscrapers can reflect the signal and make it appear to take a longer time to reach the receiver. If your receiver is picking up both the straight line and reflected signal, it can get confused and think you are moving very rapidly.

Why does my GPS receiver sometimes take a long time to find its position and at other times do so very quickly?

Your receiver needs two types of data to find its position: First, it must have a valid almanac that indicates the general locations of every satellite in the sky. Second, it must have valid ephemeris data for each satellite it is tracking. Ephemeris data is the very accurate information on a satellite's orbit that your receiver uses to calculate its position.

Almanac data remains valid for about six months. As long as you use your receiver more often than that, it doesn't have to load a new almanac. If you let the almanac get stale, your receiver needs 10 to 20 minutes to load a new almanac.

Ephemeris data remains valid for only a few hours. It should take only a minute or so to load new ephemeris data from a satellite, and it can do this for all satellites at once. Since it might not start tracking all satellites at the same time, it could take a couple of minutes to load all the ephemeris information and find its position.

If you have used your receiver in the last hour or two, both almanac and ephemeris data should be valid, and your receiver should be able to find its position in only a few seconds.

If your receiver loses track of a satellite at any time while loading ephemeris data, it has to start over. So if you travel under trees or drive under a bridge while your receiver is attempting to find its position, it can take a long time to lock on. Some newer receivers can achieve much faster acquisition times through the use of default almanacs and long-term orbits. See "The Quest to Improve Acquisition Time" on page 19 for more information.

Can I load third-party software maps into my mapping receiver?

For the most part, if you want to display maps on your screen, you must buy the software from your receiver's manufacturer. Third-party software mapping programs such as National Geographic's TOPO! or MyTopo's Terrain Navigator are designed to work with GPS receivers by transferring waypoints, routes, and tracks to your receiver and back, but they do not transfer the maps themselves. (Magellan's Triton series is an exception; they work specifically with National Geographic's maps.) If you search the Internet, you may read about creative hackers who claim to have gotten around this limitation, but that's not something the average user should consider doing.

Owners of Oregon, Dakota, or Colorado receivers from Garmin have one other option. If you can obtain a JPEG file of the map you want to load, you can use a software program called Garmin Custom Maps to upload it to your receiver. The accuracy of this approach is limited by the accuracy of the original map and by how well you can align it to specific reference points in Google Earth. Check the Garmin website at www.garmin.com for more information.

What are the best batteries to use in my receiver?

Most receiver manufacturers recommend alkaline batteries as the best overall choice. Alkalines give good life and are relatively inexpensive. They are the batteries receiver manufacturers use to measure battery life.

Cost- and environment-conscious people prefer nickel-metal hydride (NiMH) rechargeable batteries. Although initially more expensive than alkalines, they can be recharged hundreds of times. High-power NiMH batteries rated at 2,000 mAh or higher can last on a single charge as long as or longer than alkalines. Like all rechargeables, they discharge fairly rapidly even when not being used. They can lose as much as half their charge in only a few weeks, so don't use NiMH batteries in critical situations.

Another type of rechargeable battery, nickel-cadmium (NiCad), has been around longer than NiMH. They don't last as long on a single charge, and since cadmium is a toxic metal that is subject to increasing environmental regulations, the industry is phasing them out in favor of NiMH.

Lithium batteries are expensive and not rechargeable (except for custom Li-ion battery packs supplied with some receivers), but they can be useful in certain instances. They last about 30 percent longer than alkalines, but their real value is in cold weather. While other batteries quickly lose efficiency as the temperature approaches freezing, lithium batteries do a much better job of maintaining power. Here is a very rough comparison of the performance of different battery types:

Type	Relative Life per Charge	Cost	Rechargeable?
Lithium	130%	High	No
Alkaline	100%	Low	No
NiMH	60–100%	Highest	Yes
NiCad	25–35%	Medium	Yes

Appendix II

Resources

Books

Beffort, Brian. *Joy of Backpacking*. Berkeley: Wilderness Press, 2007.

Ferguson, Michael. *GPS Land Navigation*. Boise, ID: Glassford Publishing, 1997.

Jordan, Ryan, ed. *Lightweight Backpacking and Camping: A Field Guide to Wilderness Hiking, Equipment, Technique, and Style*. Bozeman, MT: Beartooth Mountain Press, 2005.

Kals, W. S., with Clyde Soles. *Land Navigation Handbook: The Sierra Club Guide to Map, Compass, and GPS*. San Francisco: Sierra Club Books, 2005.

GPS Manufacturers

DeLorme: www.delorme.com
Garmin: www.garmin.com
Lowrance: www.lowrance.com
Magellan: www.magellangps.com

Maps

www.fugawi.com
http://earth.google.com
http://maps.google.com
www.mytopo.com
www.natgeomaps.com
www.oziexplorer.com
www.trails.com
www.usgs.gov

General GPS Information

www.gpsinformation.net
www.thespacereview.com/article/626/1gps.faa.gov
www.ngs.noaa.gov/GEOID

Geocaching

www.geocaching.com
www.navicache.com
http://brillig.com/geocaching
www.geocacher-u.com
http://geocaching.gpsgames.org

Land Navigation Practices

www.globalsecurity.org/military/library/policy/army/fm/3-25-26

Glossary

agonic line The line from the North Pole to the South Pole, along which magnetic declination is zero. In the U.S., the agonic line runs from northeastern Minnesota to the Florida panhandle.

almanac A table of approximate satellite orbital information stored in a GPS receiver and used to predict which satellites should be above the local horizon.

baseplate compass A magnetic compass consisting of a circular vial containing a magnetic needle affixed to a transparent base. This is the preferred style of compass for general outdoor navigation.

bearing The direction from your current position to your intended destination. Also known as an azimuth.

bread-crumb trail *See* track log.

CEP Circular Error Probable. A measure of the accuracy of a GPS receiver based on a probability that the position reported by the receiver will be better than the CEP 50 percent of the time.

cold start The process a GPS receiver must perform to find its position when it has a valid almanac but no valid ephemeris data. (Note: Some older texts define cold start as being when your receiver has neither a valid almanac nor valid ephemeris data, but this definition has now fallen out of favor.)

coordinates The alphanumeric description of a geographic location on earth. The most common coordinate systems are latitude/longitude and UTM, but a GPS receiver can be configured for many other choices as well.

datum A model of the earth that describes it as an ellipsoid with a fixed origin and major and minor axes of specified lengths. The two most important datums in the U.S. are known as NAD 27 and WGS 84. Strictly speaking, this is known as a horizontal datum, as opposed to a vertical datum, which is used as an elevation reference.

declination *See* magnetic declination.

Differential GPS A method that uses accurately surveyed base stations and a separate transmitter to correct for GPS errors due to atmospheric distortion. The U.S. Coast Guard operates the most extensive DGPS system, but similar systems are operated on smaller scales by private companies.

DoD U.S. Department of Defense. Operates the Global Positioning System.

EPE Estimated Position Error. Some GPS receivers report this as an approximate indication of the accuracy of the current displayed position.

ephemeris The very accurate satellite orbital information a GPS receiver uses to calculate its precise distance from the satellite.

fluxgate compass An electronic version of the traditional magnetic compass.

GB Gigabytes. A measure of the amount of memory in an electronic device such as a GPS receiver.

geocaching A GPS sport in which one person hides a cache and posts the coordinates on a website. Other people use GPS receivers to locate the cache and exchange items in it.

geocoin A custom token created by geocachers and placed in a geocache.

geoid The line of constant gravity that represents mean sea level.

geostationary orbit A satellite in orbit 22,240 miles above the earth and directly over the equator. At that altitude, the satellite orbits the earth once in 24 hours—the same time it take the earth to complete one rotation. So to a person on earth, a geostationary satellite appears to remain fixed in the sky.

GPS Global Positioning System.

GPSr Slang for GPS receiver.

heading The direction you are currently moving.

hot start The process a GPS receiver performs to find its position when it has both a valid almanac and valid ephemeris data for at least four satellites.

initialization The process employed by a GPS receiver to update its almanac for the current time, satellite orbits, and geographic position when the almanac data is not valid or you have moved more than a few hundred miles from your last position.

ionosphere The upper atmosphere of the earth, ranging from about 50 miles to 300 miles above the earth's surface. Ionized particles in the ionosphere cause a significant GPS measurement uncertainty that varies greatly depending on time of day and level of solar activity.

LAAS Local Area Augmentation System. A system designed to improve GPS accuracy in the vicinity of major airports to aid aircraft during instrument landings.

latitude A line drawn parallel to the equator that measures your distance north or south of the equator.

longitude A line drawn from the North Pole to the South Pole that indicates your distance east or west of the prime meridian.

magnetic declination For a given location, the difference in direction between true north and magnetic north. Also called magnetic variation.

magnetic north The direction a magnetic compass points. A physical location in northern Canada near Baffin Island.

MB Megabytes. A measure of the amount of memory in an electronic device such as a GPS receiver.

meridians Lines of longitude.

MGRS Military Grid Reference System. A version of the UTM coordinate system.

multipath A GPS error that occurs when a satellite signal arrives at the GPS receiver from more than one path, typically because it has been reflected from a large surface such as a metal building or canyon wall. Because the two signals arrive at different times, the receiver can't easily tell which to use to measure the satellite's distance from the receiver.

Navstar "Navstar Global Positioning System" was the original name given to GPS by the U.S. Department of Defense. While it still shows up on DoD documents, everyone else calls it simply "GPS."

neatlines The borders of a topographic map.

NMEA 0183 An industry standard for communicating between a GPS receiver and other electronic equipment developed by the National Marine Electronics Association.

parallels Lines of latitude.

planimetric map The kind of highway maps sold at supermarkets and auto clubs. Planimetric maps don't indicate the nature of the terrain in any detail.

position fix The process a GPS receiver uses to calculate its geographic position on earth.

prime meridian The position of 0° longitude. It is a line running from the North Pole to the South Pole through the Royal Observatory at Greenwich, England.

PRN code Pseudo-random noise code. The binary sequence transmitted by the satellites and used by a GPS receiver to determine the time delay between when the signal was broadcast by the satellite and when it was received by the GPS receiver.

raster graphics map A software map derived from the scanned image of a paper map.

route A series of waypoints stored in a GPS receiver in sequential order. When the route is activated, the GPS receiver guides you from one waypoint to the next in sequence.

Selective Availability The method once used by the military to artificially degrade the accuracy of civilian GPS. Discontinued by presidential order since May 2, 2000.

SIS Signal-in-Space. Term used by the Department of Defense to describe the accuracy of the GPS signal as broadcast by the satellites and prior to propagation through the atmosphere.

TFT Thin film transistor. A type of display technology used in some GPS receivers.

3D mode The mode of operation of a GPS receiver in which it is tracking at least four satellites and can accurately determine its position.

topographic map A kind of map that not only shows highways and artificial features but also uses contour lines to indicate the shape of the terrain.

track log The digitized record of your exact path of travel as stored by a GPS receiver.

travel bug A geocache item intended to travel from cache to cache. Travel bugs can be identified by a bar-coded metal tag attached to them.

triangulation The method used by GPS to determine position. Also the method for determining your position on a map by plotting the intersection of compass bearings to objects in the landscape.

troposphere The portion of the atmosphere closest to the ground. GPS error introduced within the troposphere is relatively small and predictable.

2D mode The mode of operation of a GPS receiver in which it is tracking only three satellites. Positions calculated while a receiver is in 2D mode can be subject to large uncertainties and should never be relied on when navigating in the outdoors.

2drms Twice distance root-mean-square. A measure of the accuracy of a GPS receiver based on the probability that the position reported by the receiver will be better than the stated number at least 95 percent of the time. Simple rms accuracy is similar but based on a 67 percent probability.

UTM Universal Transverse Mercator. A rectangular grid used as an alternative to latitude and longitude to describe a position on the surface of the earth.

vector graphics map A software map in which features such as roads, rivers, and topographic contours are stored as digital lines.

WAAS Wide Area Augmentation System. An enhancement to civilian GPS that employs additional satellites and base stations to measure atmospheric distortions and broadcast correction factors that a WAAS-enabled GPS receiver can use to improve accuracy.

warm start The process a GPS receiver must perform to find its position when it has a valid almanac but only has valid ephemeris data for three satellites.

waypoint A description of the geographic coordinates of a particular location on earth, named and stored in the memory of a GPS receiver.

Index

About the Author

Steve Hinch has taught courses in GPS navigation to police and fire personnel, park rangers, search-and-rescue staff, and recreational outdoor enthusiasts since 1998. Born in Seattle, he grew up in the Southern California coastal city of Redondo Beach. When Steve was young, his avid rockhound parents would pack up the family and head out to remote desert locations in search of semiprecious stones nearly every weekend. These desert explorations honed his navigation skills and taught him the importance of not getting lost.

Trained as an electrical engineer, Steve has more than 30 years of management experience in the high-technology industry. He holds three patents and has written four books. He earned a BS and a Master of Engineering from Harvey Mudd College in Claremont, California. Steve has two grown children and lives with his wife in the heart of the wine country in Santa Rosa, California. He is also an award-winning photographer who specializes in landscapes of the Southwest.